BODY SCRIPTURE
A Therapist's Journal of Recovery from Multiple Personality

Barbara Hope

BODY SCRIPTURE

A Therapist's Journal of Recovery from Multiple Personality

by Barbara Hope

Rhodes-Fulbright Library

ProdCode: CSS/250/4.80/252/28

Library of Congress Catalog Card Number

00 131421

International Standard Book Number

1-55605-297-9

Copyright © 2000 by Barbara Hope

"Traveling with a Survivor" © Myrna Bouchey

ALL RIGHTS RESERVED

Printed in the United States of America

Wyndham Hall Press
Bristol, IN 46507-9460

For
Myrna Bouchey
who made the journey possible

Shirley Glubka
who blessed me with her words

and

in loving memory of Sally Buckwalter
1934 - 1995
who opened the doors of my soul

ACKNOWLEDGMENTS

I am deeply appreciative of the loving support of many friends during this journey of healing. My heartfelt gratitude to Myrna Bouchey, Jean Schild and Fran Drabick, members of my writing group, who heard me into speech with encouraging questions and profound acceptance. Without their sustaining care this book may never have come to fruition. My whole-hearted thanks to Barbara West and Marlene Barter for making me part of their family and for nourishing me in generous, faithful ways. I thank Anne Dellenbaugh for sharing her wisdom with me and for reminding me that my healing is a spiritual practice. Enduring thanks to Tony Mullaney, my Spirit Friend, whose lasting friendship is a benediction in my life. I thank Sandy Butler for her attentive listening and unfailing kindness. My thanks to Randall Kindleberger for always letting me know that she cared. Sparkling thanks to my Be-Dazzling Friend, Mary Daly, who reminds me in all ways of the Courage to Be. Many thanks to my lesbian community, Julie Arnold, Diane Bell, Pat Donnelly, Pat Godin, Eilean MacKenzie, and Cindy Sammis for helping me play and giving me an abundance of happy memories. I thank my editor, Rose Glickman, for sharpening my work with her incisive suggestions. Special thanks to the Peace and Justice Center of Eastern Maine for their generous support.

I dreamed I had a child, and even
in the dream I saw it was my life,
and it was an idiot, and I ran away.
But it always crept on to my lap
again, clutched at my clothes.
Until I thought, if I could kiss it,
whatever in it was my own, perhaps
I could sleep. And I bent to its
broken face and it was horrible. . .
but I kissed it. I think one must
finally take one's life in one's arms.

-Arthur Miller,
After the Fall

PROLOGUE

Until I was forty-eight I told this simple story of my childhood.

I was the second of two daughters born to Adele and Walter Reeves. We lived in the South End of Boston, and later moved to Norwell Street in Dorchester, renting a seven-room flat on the second floor of a green-shingled triple decker.

The neighborhood was home to Irish, Italian, and Jewish families, corner grocery stores where I bought comics three for a dime, and freight trains that whistled along nearby tracks. We lived a short distance from Roxbury, the center of a growing African-American community. Riding the trolley through the city taught me about racism in America.

My mother waitressed at a local restaurant, taking the five p. m. to 1 a. m. shift six days a week. Beloved by her customers, her work was first in her life. Family was a distant second. Her housekeeping was meticulous but her behavior was unpredictable. Frightened by her anger, threats, and humiliations, I withdrew to protect myself.

My father was a short-order cook, usually employed by restaurants, schools or hospitals. Depressed and moody, he drank beer or stared solemnly out a window. I liked the swing he hung on the back porch for me and the breakfast pancakes he occasionally made. These snippets of happy memories were diminished by my fear of him and the silence that lay between us. In my story, he was a shadowy figure who seldom lived with us. I scarcely knew him. When I was sixteen, he and my mother divorced. Three years later at age forty-seven, he died from arteriosclerosis.

My sister, outgoing and athletic, was two years older than I. Jody was a natural leader in the neighborhood. Her agile, slim body and long blond hair were a sharp contrast to my awkward, chunky, taller build and brown hair. Jody expressed her feelings directly and this startled me. She loved animals, filling her bookshelves with horse stories and bringing stray dogs to our front steps.

When we were left by ourselves we often fought, hurling words and objects at each other. She was in charge, responsible for putting the heat under the vegetables or taking the tuna plate from the fridge. I remember how she persuaded me to eat the dark beans on my plate. "Count them," she said, and I did.

In this story of my early years, I was a withdrawn child, given to solitary activities and religious devotions, finding solace in books and in the nuns whom I wanted to please - a good catholic girl. Inwardly, I had a haunting sense of being bad, different from other children. I stuttered, wet my bed, over-ate, and retreated inside myself.

This was the story I wove from elusive, scattered memories. Even in the telling, knots would grow and spread in my stomach like ragged tendrils, while inexplicable anxiety snatched at my breath and left me mute. I hid these feelings under the calm, competent persona I had managed to create. Until I was forty-seven, I told this story of my life. Then, voices - long suppressed, unsuspected - appeared to tell another story.

INTRODUCTION

> Re-membering 1: Re-calling the Original intuition of integrity; healing the dismembered Self. . . . 2: Realizing the power to See and to Spell out connections among apparently disparate phenomena. . . .
>
> (Mary Daly, *Wickedary*)

Before I went into therapy ten years ago I did not know memories were stored in my body and held by multiple personalities. Nor was I aware that my brain was marked by neural pathways forged by trauma. I was a quiet woman. I had resigned myself to living with an internal barrier, a steel door that kept me disconnected from myself and from others.

I knew I was emotionally impoverished, but I managed to do well in my work. Over the years my chosen fields had included pastoral ministry, teaching, political activism, public speaking, and therapy for battered and abused women. I was familiar with the language of trauma but did not suspect that I had been victimized.

At forty-seven I began therapy for the seventh time. Within two years I was diagnosed with Multiple Personality Disorder, renamed Dissociative Identity Disorder (DID) in the Diagnostic and Statistical Manual of Mental Disorders.*

There is a wide spectrum of dissociation. In everyday dissociation one can drive for miles and suddenly become aware of having blanked out for an hour. A similar experience can occur when one is deeply absorbed in a movie or immersed in a compelling book. In these instances the normal mental capacity to dissociate brings about an altered state of consciousness.

At the clinical end of the spectrum is multiple personality. Recent studies generally identify childhood trauma as a significant factor in the development of DID. In the growth of a healthy child, various dimensions of the self evolve and become integrated into a harmonious and complex whole. In a child burdened by chronic abuse and clinical dissociation, the self is divided into separate parts each having its own identity, memory and consciousness. These parts of the self assume their own internal and external lives with unique behavior, affect, and knowledge.

---

* American Psychiatric Association, 1994.

Dissociation and a multi-dimensional self are natural human capacities. They are not the problem. The problem is the existence of overwhelming atrocities in the lives of children which results in disabling fragmentation.

During the past thirty years women have broken their silence about battering, rape and sexual abuse. Their courage has expanded public awareness of the prevalence of trauma and alerted mental health practitioners to the primary role of trauma in causing mental illness. Their stories also have resulted in a political and scientific debate about the nature of memory. Like other survivors, I struggled with this question of authenticity, aware that memories may be fragmented, confused or otherwise distorted.

They may also be accurate.

The diagnosis of DID opened a path to my own healing. I was given a framework which helped me to understand lifelong experiences of discontinuity, depression, anxiety, and memory loss. In the course of therapy, over one hundred "alters" - separate personalities - revealed their own various and distinct memories. Their disclosures were marked by powerful emotion, physical pain and complex physiological sensations. For ten years we inched toward a cooperative internal system and integrated wholeness. As therapy deepened I came to slowly accept that, in my case, DID overlapped with an underlying mild psychosis.

I searched for myself in therapy. Discovering multiple alters was one avenue of this search. Another significant path was my relationship with the therapists who worked with me. My therapy began with Sally. I was the first person with multiple personality with whom she had ever worked. Our relationship was intense. For six years she provided a safe, nurturing environment which made it possible for my alters to identify themselves and to learn skills essential to recovery. I believe that Sally's empathy and skill built a solid foundation for the hard work of integration.

When she became seriously ill, Sally referred me to Shirley. Her spare, focused style was very different from Sally's emotional engagement. Shirley had considerable clinical experience with clients who experienced dissociative disorders. The therapeutic boundaries between us were clear and firm. Her interventions were precise and carefully rendered. We worked slowly toward integration, uncovering layers of thought, feeling, and meaning. I came to love Shirley as a wise and compassionate guide. In time, as I felt her deep acceptance of me, I could tell her everything.

During this process I maintained my practice as a clinical social worker. I discovered that one major alter functioned as therapist. This unconscious compartmentalization protected both my clients and me from any interference from other alters in the system. Over time I was able to integrate the "therapist" into myself.

The slow, spiraling process of therapeutic change in which shifts are subtle, and only gradually become lasting, is reflected in the narrative structure of this book. The process of healing might be akin to sailing in and out of a fierce storm until one learns to reduce the storm's impact by stabilizing one's craft.

I offer this record of my journey with the hope that it will give encouragement to survivors of trauma, understanding to the families and friends who love us, and inspiration to therapists who witness our suffering and healing. May all our efforts help create a world in which all children will be respected, protected and loved.

WINTER 1988

> I'm standing in a filthy room. The space is littered with papers, clothes, and dried leaves. I open a file drawer and discover old things that I had forgotten.
>
> (Dream: February 22, 1988)

I took a long look at the sea smoke curling over the ocean on that February morning, and once again, felt strengthened by the rugged beauty of the Maine coast. I set out for the ninety-minute drive for my first appointment with Sally, a therapist recommended by a friend, and felt grateful that the weather was bright and cold and that the winter roads were clear.

I felt a peculiar blend of anticipation and fear as I reviewed the problem that led me to seek therapy. I had been working at a center for battered women for three years doing advocacy and crisis counseling. When the coordinator left I became interim director. Before long, tensions developed among the small staff. The conflict culminated when a worker with a history of verbal and emotional abuse threatened to assault me. I filed a complaint requesting that she be fired, but the board of directors refused to dismiss her until they became the target of her threats six months later.

During the months of this struggle, collegial friendships became strained. I suffered depression, digestive problems, sleepless nights, and debilitating anxiety. I felt guilty and ashamed, sneaking into my office through the back door and remaining silent during board meetings. Despite constructive changes at work, the painful feelings did not subside. I finally acknowledged that the emotional tidal wave was beyond my control, and that I needed help to resolve this dilemma.

My anxiety escalated when I saw the Catholic Church where Sally and I would meet. I opened the heavy basement door. A life-sized crucifix dominated the stairway. It reminded me of suffering, my own as well as the world's.

I found Sally in a small classroom, sitting behind a long metal table. A gray coat and silk flowered scarf rested on her shoulders. Her silver hair fell in soft waves around her face. Her eyes were blue and her face deeply lined. Her voice was low, warm, and mellow. She appeared powerful, distant, and unsmiling. I felt immediately afraid.

I took in my surroundings: high walls with four basement windows, pipes running along the ceiling, a dozen or so folding chairs, and children's drawings taped on the wall. Having spent my childhood in Catholic schools I felt oddly comforted that my therapy would take place in a Sunday school classroom.

Sally listened quietly to my account of the disturbing events at the center and my feelings of anger, hurt, and betrayal. When I concluded she suggested that my therapy could focus on my responses to the situation, namely, my tendencies to withdraw and to be nice. I wasn't sure what I expected from this interview, but as we set another appointment, I felt perplexed by rising internal tremors.

All week I thought about Sally, but I couldn't remember her face. I did recall that we both had gray hair and blue eyes and I suspected that we were close in age.

Fear engulfed me as I approached the meeting room for the second time. I spoke again about the problems at work. Sally was supportive, urging me to stay attentive to my own feelings. Then, changing the subject, she said, "Tell me about your family."

I paused and breathed deeply, gathering words for the hard, familiar story. For reasons I couldn't name, talking about my childhood was confusing, always disturbing. I told Sally about my parents, my sister and me, about my mother's unpredictable, angry outbursts, my father's moodiness, and the fights and silence between them. For the first time I used the words physical abuse and violence to describe how he hit her, how both of them hit me. My words surprised me.

I admitted that fear dominated my life, a fear that separated me from my parents and distanced me from others. Haltingly I acknowledged gaps in my history. The session unfolded with a painful memory of wearing new plaid pajamas that felt cozy on my twelve-year-old body, only to have my mother and her boyfriend laugh at me.

I described my childhood dolls and lingered on one doll that had a piece missing from her head. "I'm the doll with the broken head," I told Sally, not fully grasping my meaning. Something shifted in me. I was entering old territory in new ways.

I looked at my watch. "More time is available," Sally said. "Tell me more about yourself." I told her that I entered the convent at seventeen and left at twenty; that I married at twenty-three and divorced at thirty-five; that I eventually recognized my attraction to women and now lived with Myrna, my beloved companion.

Myrna is a poet and a professor of English at a university not far from the small seacoast town where we lived. "I met her through friends and came to Maine to be with her," I told Sally. I smiled to myself, remembering how I saw Myrna running down Sandy River Beach with her shimmering kite soaring overhead; how we danced all through that night. I delight in her, in her agile mind, her love for words, in her goodness and wit, in her spiritual practice. I love her looks, her short red hair, clear blue eyes, and strong five-foot-four-inch frame. She is adventurous and fearless, compassionate and confident.

I consciously avoided discussing my four children. Sitting in this room, being listened to, I felt vulnerable and exposed. I was afraid that Sally would lash out at me, even hit me. After our meeting, I felt dazed, and moved slowly as if in a dense fog. I stopped at a supermarket and didn't recognize a friend who greeted me.

At our next session, I risked a disturbing truth. "There's a steel door inside me," I told Sally. "I've never been able to get past it; it blocks me from myself."

"Have you tried therapy previously?" she questioned.

Yes," I responded and told her the story of my earlier attempts. The first time was six months after I abandoned the religious life. I was suffering overwhelming anxiety and began weekly meetings with a psychiatrist in his Boston office; our work lasted a year.

The psychiatrist, a tall man with white hair, leaned back in his chair without looking at me. I remember feeling small and insignificant, uncomfortable in the straight-back chair next to his desk. I liked the inspiring print on his wall: a picture of St. John of the Cross and the words, "In the end, we will be judged on love." Week after week he interpreted my dreams of sexual assault as masked sexual desire and advised me to marry and have children.

Two years into my marriage I returned to him because my depression, anxiety, and sexual problems did not abate. He advised me to have more children. As I told Sally about these years in my early twenties, a sense of disconnection from my own life enveloped me.

Ten years later I was in marital therapy with my husband to clarify and resolve the convoluted maze our family had become. Initially the counselor worked with both of us, but he soon decided that I needed individual help. I was acutely distressed during these sessions, particularly when he used gestalt techniques, prompting me to move from chair to chair in response to feelings and perspectives within myself.

I terminated when he became angry because of my decision to divorce my husband, to arrange joint custody and to leave the children in the physical care of their father. "They are crying in their beds, missing you," he said accusingly. I knew he was right, but there was nothing I could do.

I sought therapy again in my thirty-seventh year when I was working in a large peace organization to protest nuclear weapons, nuclear energy, and the inflated military budget. I was also involved in feminist efforts to end sexism within the Catholic Church. Despite a community of friends and meaningful political work, I was consistently haunted by depression and thoughts of suicide. In the course of a year's work, this therapist managed to curb my despair, but she also sexually seduced me.

As this painful episode tumbled out, I felt ashamed, frightened, and confused. I told Sally how I then turned to two therapists in quick succession. Both tried to help me establish goals for my life, but neither was able to attend to my feelings of betrayal and loss. From each of them I sought help to heal emotional trauma, but I was incoherent about my feelings. Only several years later, reading an article about sexual abuse in therapy, did I recognize that this is what had happened to me.

When I was forty, a disturbing emotional crisis with Rita, my lover at the time, led me to therapy again. Lucy, with whom I worked for two years, was a warm, strong lesbian who helped me sort out my confusions in lesbian relationships and my pattern of involvement with women who were in committed relationships.

After these disclosures to Sally, I felt lighter. But I knew that there was more to unearth, even though I couldn't name it at the moment. I felt painfully aware of being emotionally blocked. As I drove home, I wondered why I was afraid of Sally. My deepest wish was to be honest with her and to make of this therapy a journey to the source of my pain, one that would give me the courage to move beyond it. I was hopeful.

Work at the battered women's center improved. We had a new director, a lesbian with seasoned feminist politics. She and her partner became friends with Myrna and me, and the four of us enjoyed great vegetarian meals and long conversations. Within a few months, another lesbian joined the staff and the three of us became close friends. In spite of these heartening changes, I wanted to pursue new directions in my work, and I enrolled at a new program in Social Work offered by the University of Maine. Sally was supportive of me and counseled that my own healing would make me a better therapist.

Between sessions my anxiety escalated. I was deeply ambivalent about what I had disclosed. Was I being disloyal to my family, exaggerating my history for the sake of Sally's attention? Were my memories distorted? After all, I convinced myself, my parents worked hard for us and did the best they could. When Sally asked about my own children, a nameless fear washed over me.

I reentered the world of marriage and children. In the course of eleven years I had six pregnancies: four healthy children, David, Stephen, Claire, and Ellen. I had one child, Susan, who died in infancy, and one miscarriage. When the marriage dissolved, I decided to leave the children in the physical care of their father. My two sons and two daughters were very young, ranging from ten years to thirty months. "I was depressed and emotionally disturbed and felt that the children would be better cared for by their father. " My voice cracked. I shook and sobbed, connecting with that catastrophic loss and deep sorrow.

Sally moved from behind the table and wrapped her arms around me. Sitting beside me, she asked, "Where did the decision to leave the children come from?"

The story tumbled out. I was depressed and angry with the children, even hitting them on a few occasions. I was terrified by my anger. At night I sometimes woke up, sensing the presence of spirits. I felt confused about myself, torn apart by something I could not grasp, as if some nameless force was pushing me from the family.

"You judge yourself harshly," Sally said. "Children can accommodate love and anger far better than denial. "The compassion on her face encouraged me to turn toward myself with mercy.

At the end of our first month I was surprised by the intensity of my feelings and at how much I had shared. She told me that she would be travelling with a delegation to El Salvador to support people who were in danger from the military. "I'm sorry about this three-week interruption. Had I known earlier I would have delayed the start of your therapy," she said with feeling.

I knew that I would miss her and worry about her safety, but a break from therapy also brought a measure of relief. I was frightened by the path I was taking and the openness our relationship was creating in me.

SPRING 1988

I'm in a war zone, terrified by exploding
bombs and men with guns. I want to cross to the
other side, but need someone to help me.

(Dream: May 5, 1988)

While Sally was gone I continued the healing process through daily affirmations, Tarot cards, and visits with supportive friends. Still, I remained enormously depressed. I took long walks on our beach, turning over broken shells, understanding that I, too, was broken.

I injured my back and, with Myrna's encouragement, treated myself to my first massage. In this quiet space, memories of my mother seeped into consciousness. I recalled how she stared into space, seemingly unaware of the world around her. I remembered how she crawled into bed with me, perhaps when I was ten, spooning herself around me. I thought about my bedroom, the tufted yellow spread, green and yellow flowers on the wallpaper, maple furniture, and a small night stand for my precious radio, where I tuned into "Lux Radio Theater," "Baby Snooks," and "Mr. Keene, Tracer of Lost Persons." I returned to my mother's body. How I hated her touch, the feel of her nightgown, her tight hold on me. Something vague and nameless about the bedroom haunted me. The past dragged me back but I wondered about the value of turning over old ground. My life with Myrna was good. We loved each other, our peaceful home on the coast, our work, and our wonderful circle of friends. Would therapy disrupt our life?

Nevertheless, I was surprised and delighted when I received a postcard from Sally. When she returned I stood by the table in our familiar room. I wanted to hug her but I held back. "I'm afraid of you," I said.

"We were moving rapidly; there are reasons why you find it difficult to trust me," she replied. Hearing these words, I felt comforted and understood. I noticed the thin black necklace she was wearing. "It was given to me by the Salvadorans I stayed with; it represents a disappeared member of their family," she told me sadly. I touched the slender strand and felt the courage woven in the threads.

She reported another story. "One morning I drove into town to get food with other women on the delegation. A soldier pressed a gun into my back." She sighed, looking away. I couldn't imagine her feelings.

I was reminded of my visit to Nicaragua in 1981 when I met with many people who endured great suffering for the sake of the Sandanista revolution. Some talked about their achievements in the literacy campaign, others identified progress in health care, and some showed me the scars on their bodies where they had been tortured by the military. Their bravery stirred me deeply. It wasn't until years later into my therapy that I understood my sense of deep connection with people who have suffered severe trauma and somehow endure.

We returned to the anger, repulsion, and fear that memories of my mother evoked in me. I felt bewildered by the depth of these feelings. Where did they come from? I remembered a moment when my mother, my sister, Jody, and I were in a bar. We were small children, perhaps seven and eight years old. My mother talked to a male friend while we sipped cokes. When we left the bar, I turned to my mother and said, "We aren't being brought up right. " My mother hit me hard, warning me not to talk like that.

Adele, my mother, often accused me of being a slob like the downstairs neighbor, or having St. Vitus Dance. She mocked me, laughing at my clumsiness. One day when I was carrying her tea to the table, she tripped me and smirked. "I avoided her," I told Sally. "She would pull down the green shades in our apartment and warn us not to tell anyone what went on inside. "

As I spoke, it became clear to me that I was never allowed to show my feelings or express my needs. In Sally's presence I began to name my fear and anger toward my mother. I didn't blame myself for these feelings. I was beginning to learn that feelings are neither good nor bad; they simply are.

I called my sister for support and for information about our childhood. In our adult lives she had been very responsive to my emotional problems perhaps because of her own recovery from alcoholism and her struggle with depression. "There was a lot of violence in our neighborhood," she said. "We could hear the screams of kids being beaten by their parents. "

She recalled how our father used his belt on us, how we were hit by a babysitter, and how both of us avoided our mother. Jody reminded me that we were shunned by our neighbors. "Don't you remember sitting in the hallways of other kids' houses, hoping someone would play with us, not wanting to go home?" Listening to her, I was dismayed by the fragmentation of my memories. The more I opened to the past, the more I felt shaken by emotional instability. On the other hand, after two months in therapy, I could finally recall Sally's face.

Without warning, my dreams intensified. I dreamt first of Sally, wondering if she wanted to sleep with me; I dreamt of a hurt child whose limbs were out of control, of a group of people telling me to keep silent, and of a baby with a raw, sore vulva. Warily, I resolved to keep a journal, intrigued by these eruptions from the unconscious.

Night after night I dreamt about violation. My father moved his hand over my naked body; an adult tied up a child, forcing her to eat feces; babies were bruised, injured, and abandoned; I was lost in dangerous places with threatening people. "These dreams are clues to your submerged history," Sally said, "markers for the journey ahead." I recorded my dreams each day, sadly aware that these very themes have always recurred in my dream life: sexual assault and chase, entrapment by threatening men.

During an April session we focused on a dream in which a young girl was raped. "Remain open to all your feelings," Sally urged. I turned away from her, closed my eyes and wrung my hands, feeling covered by filth and shame.

"He. . . he. . . he. . . . " Long silences punctuated the words. I stuttered as I did when I was a child. "He. . . he. . . put. . . put. " Anxiety gripped me. "Thing . . . thing. . thing. He put his thing in her. In me." I screamed.

The girl in the dream had a name; I was the girl and the rapist was my father. I could hardly look at Sally. "You are good," she said compassionately, "the abuse was bad. "

Sally sat next to me, waiting, listening. A part of me wanted to put a space between me and her. Another part longed to be held by her. I feared that she would get close and use my trust against me. I wondered if my ambivalent attachment to her reflected my attachment to my father.

We moved into May and explored the sexual trauma inflicted by my father and the challenges of the therapy relationship. I felt disoriented by the gap between the calm, contained woman I had become and the terrified, chaotic child who met with Sally. In my own work I had listened to other women tell stories of sexual abuse, but I never identified with their pain.

Suddenly I was confronted by my lifelong fears of genital sexuality. I remembered myself as a young woman, throwing my husband off my body, learning to endure his touch from a great emotional distance. Sally wondered if we were moving too fast, but I couldn't restrain the rush of dreams and memories.

Sally sat close to me; sometimes she reached over and held my hand. One morning, my eyes closed, gripped by fear, my fingers moved over Sally's hand, searching for some primitive connection. Sally accepted this wounded and desperate child. She let the child move her fingers back and forth across her hands. Gradually, my fingers settled and I opened my eyes, relieved to see Sally. She was Sally and more than Sally.

Sally turned my attention to the way I rubbed my legs, and held them tightly together. "Whenever you speak of your father, you rub your legs and hold them protectively." She said it was all right to comfort myself in that way.

"Go into the feelings you have when you rub your legs and allow images to surface," she suggested.

"I'm on my bed in the yellow room of my childhood, my father is on top of me, rubbing his penis against me, trying to insert himself into me." My voice escalated and my hands anxiously rubbed my face. "I can't make him stop." I held my head in my lap as the words sputtered out. My body ached. I slid close to Sally and rested my head on her lap; she gently stroked my head and rubbed my back.

Sally raised many questions about the abuse. "Did you dissociate? Did you feel you were protecting your father? Did you get caught in his feeling of depression? Did you think you could help him in some way?"

"I pitied him. I saw him look sadly out the window for hours. I heard my mother insult him and saw her pull away from him."

Sally suggested that pity enabled me to feel powerful and in control, but that it masked feelings of hurt and anger.

"I think that I shut down, that parts of me have died, that parts of me have never spoken," I responded. My panic intensified and I felt that I was pounding against the steel door. Sally wondered if panic masked feelings that I was afraid of.

"It would be better if you could let go and experience your feelings, however painful," she said. "It was not your fault; the rapist is to blame." She encouraged me to distinguish between the shame I felt as a child from feelings of worth I had as an adult. This task seemed impossible to me.

I began to accept that my father sexually abused me, that he betrayed and hurt me. In my daily routine, these thoughts flickered in my mind for a moment, then vanished. It was terribly confusing to balance the intense emotion that erupted in therapy with bouts of denial that any abuse actually occurred. I felt sadly aware that I would never again reflect on my life without some association to sexual abuse. My story was changing irreversibly.

Sally provided support and safety through these immense changes. Although I still feared that she would lash out at me in anger, she was becoming my emotional mother, the internal and external figure that I turned to for consolation.

Although Sally's kindness soothed me, I felt that it was wrong, treacherous, to reveal what Daddy did. I listened to women at the shelter reveal the horrible abuses that they suffered and I marvelled at their capacity to speak.

I, too, wanted to find words. I began to wonder who I might have been if I had not been raped by my father. Every therapy session became a fall into chaos. "Is it all right that I rest on your lap sometimes?" I asked Sally cautiously.

"It's unusual, but you're on an unusual journey," she replied. "What you have experienced is that our relationship and this room are safe for you," she said.

"Yes, but there's no continuity between sessions. It's as if I meet you every week for the first time."

"I'm here for you," she replied.

In late Spring I visited my mother. Adele was seventy years old, living with a friend in a comfortable Boston apartment. With the exception of some arthritis, her health was excellent. Awkwardly, we sat across from each other in the small den. We had never had intimate conversations. "I believe that Dad sexually abused me," I said.

She looked down. "I didn't know about it. I've seen lots of mothers on TV who didn't know it was happening in their families. If I had known I would have thrown him out." She twisted a ring on her finger, looking at me anxiously. "Did it happen when I was at work?"

"Yes, and at other times," I admitted. She asked me no further questions, but she volunteered that Walter, my father, lived with us almost continuously until we moved from Norwell Street when I was thirteen-years-old. "I thought he was absent most of the time," I exclaimed.

"Oh no, he was there," she said bitterly. "He was in the Navy for a short stint when you were four, and he left us again for some months when you were eight. When we moved from Norwell Street, we finally separated and he got his own apartment."

I was shocked. For years I had believed that he seldom lived with us. I realized that I had erased him from the family in order to bury the abuse, that my account of my childhood was distorted, and that I did not know my own history.

SUMMER 1988

I dive into deep water but suddenly fear that
I have gone down to a dangerous level and will
not surface. I swim frantically, finally
reaching air.

(Dream: August 20, 1988)

Sally invited me to draw during our meetings and I responded enthusiastically. She placed the large white paper on the floor and handed me the jumbo crayons. I sat cross-legged drawing my family, splashes of color with neither form nor face. The coloring released something in me. Drawing felt like a way out of myself and into myself. This was a peculiar discovery, for as a child I was frightened and intimidated by paint and paper. One morning, after I completed a picture, Sally asked me for a hug. I opened my arms to her, deeply affected by her warm invitation. This moment fell into my heart, consoling the wounded places.

Over the next dozen weeks I made endless drawings of myself, my family, memories of my life and images from dreams. Even as my trust in Sally became sturdier, I feared that I might be demanding too much from her, that she might push me away and insist that I grow up before I felt ready.

Sally understood and accepted my confusions and ambivalence. In these simple but powerful moments the silences in me began to find a voice.

With Sally's encouragement I felt ready to join with other Maine survivors in a weekend gathering sponsored by Looking Up, a statewide organization for survivors of sexual abuse and our supporters. About two hundred women met at a camp nestled in woods and fields. Although there were cabins to house us, I set up my dome tent, knowing my need for solitude.

In small and large groups we explored the influence of sexual abuse on our lives and the political context that contributed to violence against children. At times I was afraid of the others or overstimulated by conversations, and I retreated to my tent.

One afternoon I raced to the safe room, a protected place where counseling help was available. I didn't know why I had come and I couldn't speak.

In a writing workshop my mind raced with images of the yellow bedroom. I jotted in my notebook:

> I remember the mirror over the bureau
> the rectangular mirror
> the carefully carved frame
> the soft knobs, the twirls,
> the mirror that saw the room
> the mirror that held the memory
> the mirror I need to walk into

Returning to therapy, I read my words to Sally. "There is a voice in me that is learning to speak," I said.

"Speaking opens new doors and will lead you deeper into yourself," she said. Her eyes filled with tears. "I feel privileged to be making this journey with you; something comes back to me. I feel a certain human richness in this process."

My dreams slowly changed as disturbing episodes of violation and dramas of unruly children dominated my sleep. "Distinguish between your competent self and Barbie, your child self who is immersed in helplessness and anger," Sally urged.

The naming of Barbie, a nickname used by my mother, felt threatening to me, as if my inner world was loosening. What if this healing process unhinged the self-structure that I had so carefully built? The thought persisted that I was withholding much of what I knew from Sally; the trouble was - I didn't know what I knew.

I began to say: my father raped me. The words compelled me to hurt myself, to inflict pain. My right hand scratched and dug at my left arm. I remembered my childhood search for ways to punish myself. Jody reminded me how I peeled skin from my bleeding feet.

"In the convent," I told Sally, "we were given a metal chain with jagged edges to wear on our upper arm two days a week. Although the chain could be adjusted, I always wore it as tight as possible. Humiliation and pain were a relief." She nodded compassionately.

Together Sally and I explored my life in the convent. I began to understand that religious life provided silence and safety. I loved the hours of prayer and study, the heavy serge robes, the strong rosary beads hanging from my waist and the wide, ancient halls, polished to a high gloss. I recalled looking at the sisters as they sang hymns of praise or kissed the refectory floor, and I sensed God's love for them. Their virtue was palpable. As for me, God knew and I knew that I was bad.

Praying for forgiveness, extending my arms in the chapel, imploring the heavens for grace did not alleviate my unworthiness. What was the use of giving my life to God if he did not want it? This conviction sent me back into the world four months before my twenty-first birthday.

A few months after returning home, I visited a psychologist who had agreed to assess my suitability for the religious life. He sat behind his large, imposing desk, asking me many questions and taking copious notes. When I finished, he said, "You're running away from your father." I sprang up from the chair, tossed some bills on the desk, and fled his office.

"He was right on the money," Sally said. "The convent provided protection. You buried the pain of your childhood, and the more you try to speak of it, the harder it is to speak."

An insight formed in my mind which I shared with Sally. "I was very careful not to tell my father about my plans to enter the convent but I never knew why. Now I understand that I feared he would find me."

Summer wore on. Sally joked about her dirty gardening hands and the deep tan she had from many hours of sailing. She confided that she grew up on the North Shore of Massachusetts and spent many hours climbing rocks and walking the beaches. "I love being on the water," she said. I noted the class differences between us and how material privilege generated confidence and options. When she talked about the sailing trip that she and her five adult children were planning, I was both happy for her and sad about the limited resources I could offer my own children.

In July, I drove to Boston and revisited Norwell Street. Broken windows, boarded-up houses, and abandoned cars stood as witnesses to poverty and human misery. Our green-shingled house had burned down twenty years ago and in its place was an empty lot littered with rubbish and old tires. This is the street, I repeated obsessively, that I walked when my father was raping me. I couldn't stop the words that boomed and whirled round and round in my head. I couldn't control my quivering body.

Returning home I worked vigorously in our perennial garden, hoping that hard work and sweat would blot out the violent images and terrible memories that haunted me: my father's penis in my face; injured babies with sore mouths and torn limbs; a scarred child. I dreamt of being mute with terror, of being killed because of what I knew. My father and unknown male figures stalked my dreams. I was helpless against them.

In therapy, I sat with my back to Sally, my eyes closed, my tongue paralyzed. I slid deeper into silence. I imagined being tossed in the corner of the room, broken into pieces. Toward the end of one session a child's voice said, "You aren't going to hurt me, are you Sally?" The voice startled me, escalating my fear of disintegration. I felt distraught, disoriented, unable to name the source of the voice. I experienced myself as wandering in darkness, the depths of which seemed to swallow me.

Sally wondered if the emotional chaos was connected to rage at my father. Desperate for relief, I locked myself in the small cabin on our land and let myself feel anger toward him. I screamed, pushed him away, and in the end buried my face in my hands.

I felt stunned by the solitary character of this journey. I strolled on the beach, letting the salt air revivify me and returned to the garden where sweet peas, nasturtiums, snap ragons, and petunias soothed my senses.

Outside therapy, Myrna was a safe harbor. We took a leisurely camping trip to the Bay of Fundy, enjoyed long walks and candid talks about the complex feelings each of us had about how therapy affected our relationship. Myrna, sensing my preoccupations, felt abandoned and helpless to alleviate my pain. "I need to make some changes, to do more for myself and to not focus all my energies on you," she said. I was sad for her and angry at the way trauma spread. I gave her my full support.

As the summer ebbed away, I still rubbed my hands frantically over my legs, feeling dirty, fearful, and ashamed. "You're safe; your body is clean," Sally said. She held my hands, showing me that they were whole and strong. But I couldn't absorb her words as memories of Daddy erupted into consciousness and, with them, feelings of being filthy, guilty of a terrible sin. I tripped into a flashback: he is on top of me. I saw his friend, Frank, in the corner of the room, watching. I felt words gathering but I remained mute. "There exists in you a strong prohibition against speaking," Sally observed. "The process is not rational and we will allow it to unfold in its own time."

Before Sally left for a tour of the Soviet Union, I sculpted a clay figure of her holding me. I placed this maternal form on my bureau to nourish my healing. Myrna confided that the figure also brought comfort to her, reminding her that Sally could help me in ways that she herself could not.

AUTUMN 1988

I wander through a large, dark building with many passageways, hidden doors, and secret rooms. I feel utterly lost.

(Dream: September 8, 1988)

Anxiety exploded in my veins as memories of sexual abuse overran my mind. Each day was a struggle to survive. Despite the challenges, I began the program of Social Work at the University of Maine. I hoped that my vulnerabilities would not interfere with my studies.

As our work resumed after Sally's vacation I disclosed consuming anxiety and constant tension in my stomach. "The tension and anxiety cover feelings. I think it would help to meet twice a week," she suggested. Relieved, I also followed her suggestion to take anti-anxiety medication in extreme moments.

Over the next weeks, I tried to look at Sally when I spoke, but frequently I closed my eyes and fell into a terrible sphere of silence where words couldn't be formed. I didn't know what stirred in me during those times. It was as if some powerful force rose up and took over my being. When words came, they seemed to fall from an unknown place. Linked together, the words disclosed violent abuse by Daddy.

"He caught me in the bathroom one day and forced oral sex," I told Sally. As I spoke I felt I was actually in the bathroom, assaulted by my father, the old marble sink and claw foot tub became a blur. I couldn't stop shaking, choking.

"You can leave the bathroom now," Sally said. "Take my hand and walk out with me." We left the bathroom and walked to the clothes-lined back porch. Gradually, I returned to the present, rested on her lap, and listened to her heartbeat.

As Sally held my hands one morning, a voice said, "I'm very little. " Confusion swelled in me. I turned to Sally, and with my eyes opened, I was surprised to see her sitting close to me.

I reviewed my relationship with my father - my efforts to please and protect him, my helplessness in the face of his abuse, and my fear. My last conversation with him occurred when I was nineteen, a novice in religious life. I had written to him a few months earlier and he responded, asking if he could visit me in the convent in rural Connecticut. Arriving one May afternoon, he asked, "How could you do this, you loved life so much?" I didn't remember my response, only the knowing look on his face and a jarring perception that he knew me deeply. I was relieved when the prayer bell ended our visit.

I asked Sally if it was wrong to have loved him. She said, "Your love was a miracle and he twisted that love to serve himself."

A flashback. I stood in the small kitchen on Norwell Street. Daddy was watching me. I felt frozen in terror. He pushed me into my bedroom, hit me, separated my legs. The pain swelled. His anger felt like fire in the room. Now, in the therapy room, dreadful rage rose in me like a volcano. I shaped a clay figure of my father, threw it on the floor, stomped on it, but felt arrested by a fear which I did not understand. "You're afraid because you're taking control, a control denied you when you were a child," Sally said. "You lived in fear of your father's anger, while he deprived you of your own," she added.

I thought of how often in therapy I became a child, hands demurely folded in my lap, repeating over and over, "I'll be good; I'll be good." I began to connect my fear of my father's violence to my own fear of speaking.

"Your silence did not protect you in the past, nor will it save you now," Sally said, reminding me of the words of the Black Lesbian poet, Audre Lorde.

"Since my childhood I have had a disturbing image of my face being damaged," I told Sally. I had experienced this wounded face for many years, had felt my face covered with bruises, blood, and scars.

"Let's create an internal safe room for this child, a place of comfort and warmth," Sally suggested. She invited her to speak but the child remained silent. I believed that it was she who moved in my dream life: a swollen face and closed mouth, a wounded stomach, thighs with open sores, a frightened figure curled speechless in a fetal posture.

I felt close to this child. We told her that we were listening, that she was free to say whatever she wished.

The strain of therapy spilled over into school. During a discussion of trauma in infancy my eyes filled up; I felt dazed, almost in shock. In the library I discovered Louise Kaplan's *Oneness and Separateness*, poetic book, about the complex world of the infant. How I wished my beginnings had been cradled in safety and care, and how I wished I could have protected and cared for my own children. I hit my youngest daughter when she was two, and the blow left a temporary bruise on her face that I had never forgotten. I wondered if this event was linked to my leaving the family a few months later. I wondered if there was a connection between my abuse of her and the abuse I suffered.

I worried about my capacity for violence. I recalled that as a pre-teen babysitter, I was cruel at times, threatening to lock children in a closet. "Impulses to hurt others confused and frightened me, " I told Sally. "Even now, I sometimes drive down a road and think of running over people." My skin burned with shame. As we explored this emotional terrain, an angry child appeared in my dreams, a wild boy who needed to be caged. I reached toward this child, recognizing him as an aspect of myself. I wrote in my journal: "I feel divided all over. "

WINTER 1988 - 1989

> I'm in a house with a little girl. She
> invites me to accompany her to the cellar.
> I don't want to go, but eventually agree to
> descend the steep and unsteady steps. In the
> cellar she points to a baby in the corner and
> shows me a pair of torn pajamas. I want to leave
> but Sally joins us and we play together.
>
> (Dream: December 12, 1988)

I grappled with the conflicting emotions I felt for my father: fear mixed with love, a need for his attention crossed with a terror that I could not escape him. As memories of his abuse surfaced, I mourned the loss of him and the death of my hope for love from him. "I made myself pretty for him and felt like his girlfriend," I told Sally. I screamed and hit my body; the pain was a release. I felt that my body was riddled with splinters.

"My heart goes out to you," Sally said. "We will take out all the splinters."

Even as Sally reassured me, I worried that she might be laughing at me. I feared her anger and worried that I would disappoint her. In dreams, I searched for her but couldn't find her, or, finding her, she was too busy to be with me.

"As you let me share your inner world, you face all the losses of the past," she said. "In our relationship you have let me take care of you and have not taken care of me. This reverses a familiar pattern in your life, but causes you emotional turbulence," she added.

We explored my feelings, associating them with my mother's mockery, her general absence, and my abhorrence of her physical closeness. "Do you feel that they both wanted your body? Do you sense that your mother was trying to protect you?" I had no answers.

I did know that I avoided her, that I was repelled by her. I wondered if this had something to do with the moment in my childhood that my mother packed her bags and declared she was leaving. "Jody and I ran down the street, calling her to come back," I sadly recalled.

"That was a frightening experience for a child," Sally said. "Do you think your mother loved you initially but became angry and withholding when she sensed your father's relationship with you?" She wondered if at that point I felt her abandonment and experienced catastrophic loss. I shrugged.

I felt battered and tossed about by the ocean of feelings that threatened to drown me. "You're more than your feelings," Sally offered. I wrote on a card: "the abuse was in the past; I am bigger than my feelings; I am more than my feelings. " I placed the card on the windowsill above the desk where I worked and gazed at the ocean; the words were an anchor in the storm.

I was building a fire in the stove one cold morning when a memory flashed into my mind's eye. I was in the sixth grade lined up with my classmates for monthly confession. Father Bartholomew pulled back the sliding wood door. I confessed that I have sinned. I murmured that I have fucked. "Do you know what that means?" he asked.

"Yes," I answered. Daddy taught me." Father Bartholomew told me to say three Hail Marys and three Our Fathers and to make a good Act of Contrition. I lifted my eyes, watching him raise his hand in absolution on the other side of the grill.

"I want you to come to the rectory after school," he added. A few hours later he opened the rectory door and led me to a small parlor. Instructing me to kneel near him, he placed my hand on his genitals. His hand was strong, his skin rough. As if from a distance I heard his gravelly voice, "Your father needs you."

Sally encouraged me to file a report to the Archdiocese of Boston. I received a letter of sincere regret and learned that Father Bartholomew left Boston in the late fifties without a trace.

"What does it mean to you to have been sexually abused by a priest?" Sally asked. I thought of the priest's hands holding the Sacred Bread, the same hands that placed mine on his body.

"I feel betrayed. "

"Who could you turn to?" she asked. "Who would believe you?"

I snowshoed on trails and fields, invigorated by the exertion and the cold, nourished by winter's beauty. By day I felt calm, but my nights were dominated by fear. I dreamt that my body was dismembered; I walked through the debris of demolished buildings seeing injured babies. In one dream I washed Sally's feet; she was the healer.

As Christmas approached I grew very sad. "Perhaps you are mourning yourself, re-experiencing the grief you felt as a child who lived in a world where closeness did not exist. Christmas evokes all our deepest longings for closeness," Sally said.

"I'm always afraid that people will leave me, that I will be left alone. "

"I believe that relationships are eternal," Sally replied, "that although people go away, the connection remains. I can hold to whatever good they gave to me."

My sadness was so profound that I couldn't grasp her words. I felt catapulted back to the holidays of my childhood. My mother took pride in providing toys and gifts; my paternal grandmother required that we spend Christmas morning listening to Dickens's *Christmas Carol*. I searched for childhood pleasure in those early holidays but discovered only sadness and fear.

For the first time I had a Christmas memory of my father. I saw him putting lights on the tree, shouting at Jody and me. I saw him on the couch next to me, his hands moved over my trapped body. I saw myself crawl under the Christmas tree, sheltered by lights and branches; now I knew why I had always done this.

Myrna and I celebrated the season with a beautiful tree adorned with lights and shining ornaments. The house was festive, warmed by the wood stove and the delicious aroma of holiday cooking. We prepared for the visit of my teen-age daughters by filling their stockings, wrapping their gifts, and planning a menu that teen-age girls would enjoy - - variations of pasta and pizza.

By this time in therapy I was sensitive to the danger of family secrets, the ways that unresolved issues in one generation are passed on to the next, replicating family patterns of dysfunction. Sally encouraged me to tell my daughters about the abuse, explaining that telling the secret promotes healing and prevents abuse from happening again.

I sat at the small round dinner table with Myrna and my daughters after a hearty meal of spaghetti, waiting for the words to gather in my throat. "There's something I need to tell you," I said. I glanced briefly at Myrna for strength, then at my daughters. "My father sexually abused me when I was a child. I think that the abuse went on for a long time." I wanted to slip through this moment, forget that I was telling my daughters that their grandfather raped me, that their world was changing. They responded with love; each of them offered words of sympathy and reached for my hands across the table.

I drove on icy winter roads twice a week for my meetings with Sally. Whereas I once believed my father was largely absent from my childhood, now he was central to my memories. I reached for my baby book and discovered that my mother recorded my attachment to him. If he had loved me, how could he have hurt me? I thought of the abuse and vacillated between belief and doubt.

This struggle became acute when I suddenly remember that my father took me to his friend, Frank. I remember Frank's bare rooms at the hospital where they both worked. I felt the chill as they undressed me, the pain of their touch. As I told the story, I shivered again. I slapped my hand, accusing myself of being bad. "They were sick men who knew nothing of your feelings," Sally said. I covered my face. I felt filthy. "The dirt belongs to them," she added. Her voice came from far away, "You kept the secret, but he did not. "

With some trepidation I participated in a survivor's workshop with Laura Davis. Our twenty-member group met in a large comfortable room where we sat on chairs and pillows arranged in a circle. I wanted this experience to be healing, but it was an earthquake. I was afraid of the group and spent time alone in an adjacent room.

During one exercise I broke into uncontrollable sobs. I couldn't speak. I told the women that "I go away when I am afraid. Someone else controls my body. The woman crying and hiding is not me. My emotions switch very quickly; one feeling state replaces another without connection." I heard myself say those words but had no understanding of their significance.

As I reviewed the day with Sally, she pointed out that I had taken some risks and suggested that I join a survivor group. It was an alarming prospect. Did I have the courage to expose myself to a whole group of people and another therapist? I also wondered if Sally was pushing me away. "You associate me with your father," she said; "your fear of me is linked to your fear of him. Try to think of me as a peer on a journey that we take together. "

Sally asked me to consider whether anything was good in the relationship with my father. "I felt special and wanted to please him. He joked about taking me to Arizona because of my allergies. I liked the attention he gave me, and I liked wearing his large ring on my finger. "

I started to tell her how I rubbed his back, but the playful memory changed to dread and I fell mute. "All the feelings are true; you can hold them together," Sally encouraged me.

During a discussion of childhood trauma in a class at school, I said aloud to my classmates, "I was sexually abused by my father. " The words came out slowly, carefully. I contained the feelings that boiled within and the moment passed without any spilling over.

I described the event to Sally. "You did well," she said. Although I couldn't connect the adult woman who studied with the child who rested on Sally's lap, I was pleased. She believed, as I did, that openness about personal issues was an important component of professional development for social workers. The first anniversary of our work held sprigs of growth.

SPRING 1989

I am driving in a devastated city.
Buildings have crumbled into rubble; roads
are ripped up. I drive in deep mud. The place
is so desperate that I want to pass quickly,
but the mud is deep and the car moves slowly.

(Dream: March 5, 1989)

I began to draw more, pictures of frightening snakes and sharp knives. I felt a gaping hole in me, large enough to swallow me.
"Lean into your feelings, move with them, surrender to them, and you'll come out the other side. This is how healing happens," Sally urged. Sally planned a two-week vacation. She also urged me to find a group. Convinced that she was trying to get rid of me, I sank into depression. I hated my dependence on her, but I couldn't let go. Days before she left, these feelings escalated into a crisis of abandonment. I felt ashamed. "Be grateful for your pain," Sally said; "it will make you sensitive to the pain of others." We explored my experiences of people leaving me and my loss when I left my young children.
I did not leave suddenly. For months I had been despondent, torn between my responsibilities for my children and a growing belief that I should leave, that they would be better off without me. I wept long and often. I moved like a sleepwalker, overcome by a force that I could not resist.
"A critical reason for your leaving was your refusal to be sexual with Phil after he assaulted you," she suggested.
As she spoke I remembered the October night that he hit me. I had taken our older son to a Cub Scout meeting and cleaned up the house when we returned home. Phil arrived later, having taken the younger children to visit his parents. He was drunk, angry, and tired. He began to hit me in the living room. Surely, I told myself, he has just slipped; this was some terrible mistake.
I was wrong. He followed me into the bathroom and continued to hit me, pushing me into the tub. He threatened to kill me. When he grabbed me the last time, I broke free from my sweater and ran out the door.
Sally's voice called me back to the present. "You were unconsciously aware that the sexual abuse by your father was connected to your mother's

refusal of him." Sally was right. Remembering how she pushed him away, I felt furious. I began to see how I held my mother at least partially to blame for his abuse. Sally continued, "You feared that if you refused your husband, he would turn to your daughters. By leaving, you would break the dreaded triangle. " Her words shone a light on what had been dense, tangled, and obscure.

We went deeper and Sally's words freed me. "You felt compelled to leave because of the abuse you suffered, because you feared the children would be hurt, because you feared you might also hurt them; you were able to leave because of your capacity for pain. " I took her words to my heart, applied them like salve on terrible wounds, and felt compassion for the young mother I was.

While Sally was away I visited my younger daughter in Boston. I hated the city's noise and density. When I met Ellen her at her home, an odd, old fear gripped me and I struggled for composure as a fuzzy picture snapped into focus. I was seventeen and visiting my father in New York. While he and Jody went dancing I went back to his apartment after a brief walk around Times Square. When he returned home alone, he called me his girl. Then he raped me. "I was apart," I told Sally, "somehow there and not there at the same time."

In quick succession memories filled gaps in an earlier visit with my father in New York when I was sixteen: our meal in the Polka Dot restaurant; seeing "No Time for Sergeants", and finally, standing in a hotel shower all night. Now I knew why I needed that cleansing.

I felt sick, devastated. "He raped me." I screamed and pounded the table. Sally took my hand and rubbed my sore fingers. I remembered that when he came close to me I knew what he wanted. Sally thought that I kept it a secret from myself, at least some of the time.

I revisited my teen years. I looked back at an awkward adolescent, physically constricted, and non-athletic, who read devotional books during class recess and attended church several times a week. I sometimes went to the movies with a few friends, shopped downtown, or skated at a local rink. My heart set on religious life, I rarely dated. I did not question the peculiar feelings that set me apart from my classmates. I told Sally how guilty I felt when I was awarded a Mary-like medal at my Catholic girls' high school.

There were two parts to your life," Sally observed, "the good, gentle girl, and the hidden underside that fueled your sense of badness. " I felt great compassion for the confused adolescent that I was, so anxious that at times I was incontinent.

One morning in April, Sally announced that she wanted to limit the length of our sessions. For over a year we had been meeting from one to two hours; now she suggested that we limit ourselves to seventy-five minutes twice a week. "I want to take better care of myself and I believe that this change will be positive for us," she said.

Her words were catastrophic. I walked out in a fury. I realized how deeply she could hurt me, how much power I had given her.

For the next few days I was consumed by these hard emotions. When we met again, I sat on the opposite side of the room. "You are just like Daddy. You use your power to get what you want. You tricked me, made me trust you and need you." I folded my arms across my chest.

"This is about separation. I did not anticipate the depth of feeling this change would evoke in you," she replied. I felt an opening in our symbiotic circle of warmth and protection turning me toward my own separateness. In our relationship I experienced an odd discontinuity and a fear of both closeness and distance, trying desperately not to hurt her or provoke her anger toward me - old, familiar feelings.

"I'm afraid that you'll leave me," I said.

"I'm here for you. You are free to use our time together as you wish. When the time comes, we'll change our relationship together."

Painful as the process was for me, I felt consoled by her words. As I rested in her lap she reminded me that our relationship was different, but also the same. We acknowledged that we loved each other, but I knew that a precious chapter had ended.

I sensed that I was falling into a widening crack that I could neither hold together nor escape. My hands raced over my legs. There were no words for this. I was thrown back into my father's betrayal of me. I loved and trusted him, depended on him and wanted him to love me. Without him I did not exist. "You continued in the relationship because you needed him, because he was your world," Sally interpreted. She held my hand and told me that I was somebody. I barely grasped how I loved him, feared him, needed him. I slipped into thoughts of dying and drew pictures of blackness, emptiness, nothingness.

I worked with finger paints, using bold colors to make images of the life and death struggle of a terrorized child. "The pictures aren't horrible enough," I told Sally. I drew a child in the depths of a well praying to Jesus. There was a crucifix on the wall; the child imagined herself in a wound, held by Jesus. The well was a place of safety. No one could reach her at this silent depth.

In May, I travelled to Boston because my children's father had been diagnosed with cancer. The prognosis was poor. He was brave, committed to helping himself live. I looked at him lying in the hospital bed and my mind somersaulted over the years we shared. We never imagined who we would become. I returned to the family home, finding remnants of myself in every room, noting how little had changed in fifteen years. I was surprised by a sensation of different levels in me: an outer functioning presence and an inner disturbed shadow. I leafed through the photo albums and saw the gaping holes where in rage and grief he had ripped out pictures of me. The holes accused me. I was the woman who tried to make a home. I was the woman who felt compelled to leave. I was the woman who loved her children. I was the woman who said goodbye.

I talked with Sally about my children and my inability to help them through painful episodes in their childhood. "I had so little patience at times, so little understanding of them and their needs." I talked about the years in which I regularly took my older daughter to the dentist for braces. We could have had pleasant times on the long rides, but I was often tense and worried.

"Try to forgive yourself; try to accept that during that time you were stuck in a pattern of denial and minimization," she offered compassionately. As I considered my children's grief and saw the cloud of my own life over theirs, I glimpsed how my father's hands changed my history and the lives of my children. I resolved to use all my strength to heal the trauma in our family.

SUMMER 1989

I'm caring for a hurt baby, trying to find
food, clothes and medical help. I'm frightened
by her needs. A woman is watching us, wanting to
help. The baby asks me to believe what she is
telling me about herself.

(Dream: August 13, 1989)

Summer brought relief. I turned toward the earth, expanding the rock garden, planting phlox, pansies and sweet alyssum, and breathed in the faithful gifts of nature. With Sally's encouragement I took a solo camping trip, pressing myself to hike beyond my limits, to move beyond my fears. Each step up Mount Battie pulled something from me and gave something back. I was the child who was afraid; I was the woman who was strong. I searched to know myself through my body. I knew that the disconnection from my body made it possible to distance myself from the abuse. Having been deaf to the signals of my own flesh felt like a grievous deprivation. I reached the summit overlooking beautiful Camden harbor; a cooling wind tempered the heat and I was reminded that pain, like heat, could be transformed.

In therapy, I often noticed how I retreated in conversations with Sally. I didn't understand what caused these abrupt shifts. "When you block facing the abuse, you give it control," she warned, "while remaining open and accepting, gives you control." She went on. "There seem to be two selves in you. One, who is calm and competent, obliterates the abuse; the other remembers the abuse and feels hurt and confused."

The distinctions became sharper in a short-term, self-help survivor group. Four of us met bi-weekly for sharing and support. The experience generated high levels of anxiety in me. Someone else took control of my body. A child spoke, "I was always afraid. It was dangerous at my house. Daddy hurt me in the dark." As she rubbed her face and legs she appeared terrified. She was in and out of the meetings with alarming speed, and sometimes talked about herself in the third person. "Her legs hurt. Her mouth hurts," she said. I didn't understand what was happening, but I couldn't deny that it was real. The other women were empathic and attentive. While those meetings were painful and confusing, they helped me accept that what was happening in therapy was real, not simply generated by my relationship with Sally.

Sally encouraged me to extend compassion to myself, to love and protect the abused child that I was. I took time during the week to hold and nurture my younger self, to accept her feelings and experiences. I felt that I was on the brink of something, that I was searching for parts of myself. I began to connect the frequent feeling that "nothing ever happened to me" with a child's dissociation from overwhelming pain. One evening Sally mentioned incest and a voice shouted, "Don't say that. " I didn't know whose voice was shouting.

In mid-June Sally and I saw each other unexpectedly at a peace conference. Because we were therapist and client, we deliberately avoided any encounter. When we talked about our experiences Sally acknowledged that it had been difficult for her. "I was aware of your emotional struggles and I worried about you," she said.

"I was concerned that your perceptions about me outside therapy would affect our relationship in negative ways. Do you still like me?" I asked.

"More than ever," she replied. I'm reassured and we agreed that if overlaps occurred again, we could be easier with one another. We discussed our common commitment to peace work. "That's a very strong bond between us," Sally said. "Do you think that your efforts to promote non-violent change are a way for you to work through your childhood?" she questioned.

"Perhaps, but not consciously. When I was in the fourth grade the nuns said that the Korean War would become another world war. I knew about the A-bomb and feared the end of the world. Newsreels showed the devastating impact of war on people and countries. I was fifteen when the Suez Crisis threatened and I felt deeply that war was not the answer. The strength of my feelings surprised me. Perhaps they were also a protest against the violence that was done to me. I don't really know. As a child I often prayed for peace. "

"Peace work is a consistent thread in your life. We'll return to this again," she responded.

While Sally was on vacation, I drew pictures of the apartment on Norwell Street. I was amazed at the precise images of wallpaper, furniture, and linoleum that emerged on the page, how every inch of that space seemed burned into memory.

When Sally returned, I spread out the papers. I covered the pictures of the bathroom as if it were a dreaded space. I heard my voice talk about terror, about Daddy in the bathroom. I trembled. Sally held me and rubbed my back. "You'll gain more control of memories as time goes on, and you'll be better able to attach feelings to experiences," she said. I felt crazy, but Sally assured me that I was sane, that I was holding myself together through this process.

"Keep the abuse in the context of long ago and surround your pain with the safe self. Fear has a battering effect," she commented.

Our discussion turned to how I learned about sex. I knew about sex but didn't know how I knew, and I didn't want anyone to know that I knew. I remembered standing outside my parents' bedroom. I felt that it was a dirty, terrible place, a room that I didn't want to enter.

I told Sally how I sat in the back hallway with the boy downstairs when I was about five years old. He showed me his penis and I was amazed that it was so small. I returned to a moment in my eighth year when an older boy pushed me down on his sister's bed and tried to pull down my pants. I was terrified because I knew what he planned to do.

Later in my teen years, I asked an older girl about sex. Again, I pretended ignorance, sliding over an inner awareness of what I actually knew but needed to keep hidden. My words raced. Daddy raped me. Forced me. No way to escape from the powerful Daddy. In my panic, I disclosed recurring fantasies of violent sex. "The fantasies are the residue of your experience," Sally said. "Your feelings are strong because they were buried for so long. " She opened her arms to me, saying that I needed comfort, and that it had been a long time in coming.

I became more aware of how I had internalized my father. I began to unravel a central predicament: there was no difference, no separation between my father and me. Sally added more insight. "Your loving behavior toward your children was real, but you somehow believed that your goodness was false and the inner monster, your father, was real. "

I noticed that every time I spoke of my father's death, I wanted to die. "He took your will from you; part of you wants to deny the abuse and the fact of his death," she explained. I feared him and my anger toward him.

When I was trapped in a memory, overcome by his power, Sally taught me to shrink him in order to gain mastery over him. She helped me see that I took in my father's suffering and in the process denied my own. I learned to shout at him, stamp him underfoot, and make him disappear. I was trying to say goodbye.

He died in June, 1960. My sister came to the convent to deliver the news. We stood together in an austere convent parlor. I turned from her. She urged me to face her, to say something. I felt stunned. Even now I don't recall any words I might have spoken. She left quickly and I immediately returned to the schedule of meditation, dinner, and evening conference. After night prayer, I knelt beside the novice mistress and disclosed that my father had died. "Did you love him?" she asked.

"Yes," I murmured.

"Because your parents are divorced and your father wasn't Catholic you won't be allowed to speak about his death or go to his funeral," she said. She traced the sign of the cross on my forehead and said goodnight. The next day a sign appeared on the community bulletin board requesting prayers for a special intention. I believed that the notice referred to my father, the repose of his soul, and the family's loss. Months later the novice mistress commented that I was never the same after his death. I didn't ask what she meant, and I didn't know myself.

I feared my anger toward my father as well as other aggressive impulses. I told Sally that I still had intrusive thoughts of hurting people, that, unbidden, these thoughts invaded my mind. "I imagine assaulting people, even killing them."

"You have excellent impulse control. You haven't hurt anyone. The thoughts are connected to what was done to you," she explained. She wanted me to accept and integrate my aggression and to define it as good, but I was afraid. I resisted her suggestions to shout obscenities. I felt the need to maintain strong control; I feared further shattering.

In late summer I spent a happy day with my sons in Harvard Square. We had a wonderful time in the bookstores and lost ourselves for hours pouring over new and old texts. In the evening we gathered for dinner in the house where they were raised. We sat at the familiar black table in the center of the large, red braided rug that I made. Everything was still the same: the inexpensive prints I hung on the walls in 1969, the plaid chair cushions I had carefully sewn, the graceful antique tea cart between the windows, and the oak sewing chest Phil had refinished.

At first we just chatted. Steve, 22, regaled us with stories of life in Southern California, and David, 24, talked about his engineering work in Nevada. I listened with pleasure, adding my own tales of life in Maine. But anxiety built in me.

I waited for a pause. " My father sexually abused me when I was a child. " The moment left me exposed and vulnerable.

"I'm sorry that happened to you, but what does it have to do with me and Steve?" David asked.

"The abuse had a major impact on my life and significantly affected my mothering of you," I answered. "I think it's important to end secrecy and silence in family life in order to break the cycle of abuse." I wanted to tell them that I loved them, that my leaving them was rooted in a complex history that even I didn't understand, but I couldn't find the words.

My younger son sat silently and attentively. When we left the table, he hugged me tightly, his tall six-foot-four inch frame felt like a comfortable pillow. "My friends say that I'm a good hugger. I learned it from you," he said. Steve's words were a beautiful gift. As I carried dishes into the kitchen, I knew that we had come a bit closer to one another and had taken a first step on the road to healing.

One evening Sally surprised me with three beautiful dahlias from her garden -- rose, red, and yellow. "I want to honor your courage," she said, "and the strengths that you've developed in proportion to the abuse." I told her about a decision: to change my last name to Hope.

I had been thinking about changing my name for many years, but hesitated for the sake of my children. As they became adults I could no longer see any compelling obstacles. One night, drifting off to sleep, I asked myself to what family I belonged. The answer was the family of Hope. I knew this was the name I wanted. By choosing Hope I wanted to affirm my identity with people who committed themselves to bringing peace and compassionate justice into the world, even in the face of despair. Maybe I was ready for this name because my therapy with Sally was giving me hope. "That's quite a change," Sally said, "quite a choice."

AUTUMN 1989

> Sally and I are sitting in a large room at some
> distance from each other. I move toward her but
> when I try to talk a piece of cloth comes over
> my mouth and around my neck. I cannot speak.
>
> (Dream: September 24, 1989)

I began my second year of social work studies with a deepened understanding of trauma. In school I studied incest, at work I listened to clients who disclosed memories of sexual abuse, and in therapy I grappled with my own turbulent process of recovery.

My drawings continued to depict hideous snakes and sharp knives. I couldn't bear to look at them. "You have spent many years keeping the inner wall in place," Sally observed, "and we'll move slowly to take it down."

Increasingly, other voices filled the therapy room shouting "stop" or "don't say that."

"Who is speaking?" Sally asked. No one answered. I wondered if these were the same voices that emerged in the survivors' group last Spring.

I dreamt of a crying child covered with mud. She was naked; her hair was matted. I felt compelled to make her real. I found pieces of wood, lengths of string, and a lump of clay. Her arms and legs were thin sticks held by string to the oddly shaped wood head and torso. I pressed the clay onto the wood to form her face, her large eyes, and open mouth. Strands of brown yarn served as hair. My hand grabbed the red marker, drawing streaks of red on her legs, arms and chest. I called her Mud Girl. I didn't know what drove me to do this, or what the figure meant. I showed her to Sally. I could scarcely look at the broken face and twisted body. When I did, I wondered if she was the bruised child in me whom I had kept silent.

"You speak of her in the third person," Sally observed. "Perhaps this is a way of distancing yourself. Mud Girl was violated by the incest and by the silencing."

Sally wondered who was stifling her voice and I wondered if it was my father in me.

"He's an asshole," a voice shouted. I pushed Mud Girl off the table and turned from Sally. She suggested that I explore what Mud Girl felt and needed, that I become her therapist.

I sat with Mud Girl on the beach and she asked me to write down and remember what she dictated. "I was raped by my father. I cried by myself many times; no one helped me. I felt angry and dirty. I went away. " I told Mud Girl that I loved her, that I was listening.

Sally suggested that we use the blackboard to write out a dialog between me and Mud Girl. I picked up the chalk and wrote. On one side the writing was neat and controlled. I asked Mud Girl questions about what happened to her. She answered with profanities in large, explosive script. Sally observed that both parts are good and strong, but wondered what prevented a free flow of feelings. "Is there a trigger in you that causes you to go away?" she asked. I turned from the board, and covered my face, afraid of what I did not know about myself.

In September I decided to have a birthday party to celebrate my forty-nine years and my new name. Myrna and I decorated the house with lavender streamers and balloons. Our friends gathered at our home, and we drove to a nearby nature walk that wound through woods and ended on large, red, coastal rocks. It was a sunny fall day and the wind was brisk. We huddled together sharing a hearty lunch, matching our happy spirits with the dance of ocean waves.

I made another doll, large and soft, clothed in an infant's sleeper. She didn't want a mouth because it was too dangerous. I called her Baby. Sally removed a button from her jacket and gave it to me. "It's never too late to have a happy childhood." I pinned the button on Baby, hoping that she would heal. During therapy I held Baby, finding comfort for myself even as I comforted her.

One Friday morning I shared with Sally a vivid memory of my parents when I was a small child. My mother was cooking at the brown stove. My father approached her from behind, putting his arms around her. She shrugged, pushing him away. I was angry at my mother for not accepting him and angry at my father for always wanting sex. I felt conflicted and excluded. "He was invasive; she had a right to resist him," Sally commented.

A voice shouted, "Don't say that." I immediately apologized and turned my back to Sally, confused by my feelings.

"You feel I have left you because I defended your mother," Sally responded. She was right, I did feel hurt by her distancing. "Most of the time I attend to your feelings, but it is also important to maintain separation, knowing that we can come back together. You're having a child's feeling."

It became clear that for me both closeness and distance were difficult. I began to recognize that distance meant total separation and closeness meant unconditional connection. I couldn't hold them in the same hand. "Our relationship is solid. This is very hard work," she reminded me. I wrote in my journal that when Sally distanced from me, I felt shame and a deep sense of my own badness.

I was preoccupied with the question of closeness and distance. I recognized that Sally might not always be there for me, even though she might want to. I needed to care for myself with that same compassion. I was trying to learn that we can be separate and connected at the same time. "Secure attachment is the basis for separation," she said, " and it is the quality of the attachment that matters. "

Memories broke into consciousness: Daddy and I in the green Pontiac, in the yellow bedroom, in the empty diner on Saturday mornings. "Memory is a kind of gift that returns you to yourself," Sally said softly.

She encouraged me to talk with Myrna and close friends about my history, but the words stuck in my throat.

"Why is it so difficult to confide in your friends?" she asked. I wonder if I feared that in talking I would lose myself. I sensed that I have integrated myself with the secret intact and that speaking of the trauma threatened me in a fundamental way. I wondered if it was a fear of not knowing how others, even Myrna, would respond. I felt raw and exposed in this conversation. Sally pointed out a double bind. "If you talk, you feel your pain more keenly; if you don't talk, you feel isolated and disconnected." She encouraged me to make a drawing that included the self who withheld and the self who extended in trust. As our discussion ended, I came to the realization that I was inevitably alone. Sally nodded, "It's a bitter pill to accept aloneness. "

In late October, I gave Sally the gray wool sweater I had knit for her. The sweater featured white, rose, and blue designs. As the session opened, I hesitated, shy about offering this gift. Finally, I murmured that I had something for her and gave her the unwrapped box. She opened it slowly, smiling at me. "It's beautiful," she said, holding it in front of her. "I'll keep it forever as a reminder of you and the work we're doing together. "I couldn't stop smiling,

One November morning Sally suggested that we create a genogram of my family. She spread the large white paper and colored markers on the table. The process of diagraming my family and our relationships was both painful and enlightening. Sally drew the figures, marking dates of birth, marriage, children, death, divorce, signs that indicated alcoholism and physical and sexual abuse, and broken or strong lines which defined different kinds of relationships. My family came to life on this page, a series of separate, unrelated presences, barely connected, but weighed down by multiple losses, alcoholism, abuse, and lifelong hard work. Complicated divisions emerged, conflicts which had persisted over the years, and very few solid attachments.

I examined the drawing and saw my struggles in the context of my family history. I gained a new respect for the women in my family who endured through arduous times. I linked my capacity for hard work to my foremothers and my emotional conflicts to the legacy of loss, abuse, and disconnection that shaped my family. "Please take the genogram home," I asked Sally. "It is too difficult to absorb for more than a short time. "

Despite all the work we had done, most of my childhood felt locked away. I wondered about the voices that unexpectedly rang out. I sensed that there were voices in me that had not yet spoken. I walked out into the cold November night thinking of the scared and abused children I met in my dreams. In one dream a woman offered me a rope so that I might descend down the side of a hill, toward a bottom I couldn't see. I took the rope knowing that it was a descent into madness.

WINTER 1989-1990

> I am in a prison cell. I hear the voices
> of women and children who are being tortured.
> I see a little girl with bruises on her body. She
> tells me that it is over.
>
> (Dream: January 19, 1990)

Looking back on two years of therapy I felt stunned by the outpouring of memories and shaken by the powerful feelings that had erupted. I felt split apart and baffled by this process with no inkling of what might unfold. I held Baby, my doll, frequently now, and rocked her in my arms to comfort myself. Sally held me, stroking my head, but I knew that she couldn't take away the pain. In early winter I dreamt that I was walking on a road that crumbled beneath me, becoming a mass of holes, sharp stones, and rubble - a metaphor for my experience.

Sally asked, "In addition to being troubled by actually hitting your children, have you ever had thoughts or fantasies about hurting them?"

An unfamilar voice admonished, "You've gone too far, Sally. "

The speaker vanished. I felt crazed. In the next session, the same voice announced that she was Big Barbie. "I take care of the children inside in order to protect Barbara. I've been around for a long time," she said.

Sally asked Big Barbie whether there were others inside. "They prefer to introduce themselves," Big Barbie responded.

At home, Big Barbie created a wire doll dressed entirely in black, an image of another internal person, one to be feared. Sally wasn't surprised, having suspected such a figure in me. I felt utterly confused by Big Barbie's existence, but before I could sort this out, Daddy's Girl materialized. She was four-years-old.

"Daddy played his banjo and I sang," she confided to Sally. She burst into a chorus of "Bell Bottom Trousers. " Daddy's Girl was a sensual child who enjoyed the feel of her skin. "I like to dance and have fun with Daddy, but I don't like it when playing hurts. "

Within a week, Little Barbie, a spirited eight-year-old emerged as well. "I hid from Daddy," she said. Little Barbie found refuge in the out-of-doors and liked to explore the neighborhood. "There were grasshoppers along the railroad fence; I put them in a jar and poked holes in the cover. "

I asked Sally what these voices meant and she used the word dissociation. "Perhaps you are like a large house with closed-off rooms that are now opening," she explained.

I felt that the process was unconscious, that what was unfolding was beyond my capacity to control. In the midst of this chaos I was troubled by images of assaulting Sally. She wasn't surprised by my anger. "There are good reasons for you to feel anger," she said. "Now that you're learning about the team inside, you can draw on their strength and energy to help you grow."

In the therapy hour I learned that voices could come and go, but that I could safely return to the present. Sally told me that my selves were ways of organizing reality.

Sitting in the therapy room, my head ached, my vision blurred, and a dreadful feeling of falling apart seized me. Was I learning things that were meant to be forever forgotten? "All the selves are you," Sally urged.

My sexual relationship with Myrna became stressful. "It's too hard to make love right now," I explained. My eyes filled. "Holding, hugging and kissing are fine," I said. She took me in her arms and I felt the sadness between us.

At school I couldn't concentrate. In the class on substance abuse, images ran like a roller coaster through my mind: my father, my mother's friends from the restaurant, my sister, and my children's father - all alcoholics. Exploring the nature and consequences of alcoholism helped me understand some of the forces at work in my family. The instructor encouraged me to write about my family and to participate in class discussion, but I couldn't speak. My voice was buried in the bottom of a deep well.

My silence grew deeper when a visiting lecturer told the class that persons with dissociative disorders are also likely to receive a diagnosis of borderline personality. I knew from the literature that this was serious business. People so diagnosed were often demeaned. I remained silent, lest I expose the scars I bore.

I returned from one therapy session and collapsed on the couch. "What's wrong?" Myrna asked, putting her book down.

"There are different parts inside me," I stammered. "Sally calls them alters. They have their own names; they talk about things that I don't remember. Sally says that they're parts of me who have their own history and memories. They helped me cope with trauma."

Myrna was silent. Her body tensed. "Can you tell me anything more?"

"It's too disturbing. "I couldn't talk about it right then, even to the woman I deeply loved.

At home the physical work of bringing wood in from the outside to warm our home felt direct and satisfying. I watched sprightly chickadees and red-tailed squirrels visit our feeder. I created Solstice gifts for friends, and enjoyed trimming our eight-foot tree. All the while Odetta's rousing spirituals filled the house. When our lesbian community gathered for our annual holiday party, I felt new hope.

In February, I attended a weekend workshop with other women who had survived sexual abuse. I imagined that the company of other women would enable me to give and receive support. But when I arrived at the lovely refurbished farmhouse in the generous hills of western Massachusetts, I tried to be invisible and clung to the periphery of the group.

The evening session began with blaring music and soon the other participants were shouting rage at their abusers. Screams of "Stop! Don't! Go Away! I hate you!" broke out. I ran to a corner of the room and covered my ears.

Beth, a staff member, invited me to sit down. She surrounded me with pillows. Eventually I heard my own voice join with the voices of the other women shouting, "Stop! Stop! Don't!" In panic I rubbed my face and a voice said, "I am bad. I am bad. " Beth held my hand tightly, urging me to stay with her. Later in bed I barely slept, jarred by internal chaos, headaches, pain in my vagina and multiple images of Daddy overtaking me.

In the morning I joined the group for meditation, sending healing energy to my chakras, bathing each center with light. The process soothed and strengthened me. I walked outside in the cold dawn air renewing my commitment to this journey. I began to recognize the texture of my fear: if I open myself to the group, they would consume me and betray me. I worked to overcome this dread, reminding myself that the group was safe, that they would help me face my pain.

When we gathered after breakfast, my resolve faded. I couldn't look at anyone. Rageful voices emerged from my mouth; their power frightened me. They shouted that I was bad, that it was bad to talk. Other survivors told me that my father wanted me to be silent, but now I could talk.

I showed Baby to the other women, saying that now I felt ready to create a mouth for her, that perhaps it was safe for Baby to speak. In the evening I wrote a letter to my younger selves, appreciating their strengths, acknowledging that I survived because of their courage. I felt loving toward these parts of myself that I was beginning to know, and fell into a deep and restful sleep.

I sat with a therapist on Sunday morning, telling her about my work with Sally and my new awareness of inner parts. She spoke gently to me, "All parts of you need love; some parts may be afraid to give and receive love, even afraid of obliteration." Her words were like the noonday sun, sharpening both light and shadow. I left the weekend feeling more aware of my inner world, the shape and content of which I could only dimly perceive.

I was eager to see Sally after her two-week absence. At the same time, I didn't trust the continuity in our relationship. My anxiety dissipated as we reviewed the workshop, my feelings of fragmentation, as well as moments of grace and transformation. "You were open to the process," she observed, adding that "when you tear down a layer in yourself, you are able to experience deeper communion with others. "Sally said that I looked different, that the workshop appeared to have been a spiritual experience, a gift of faith.

The compartmentalized life I was leading perplexed me. In my daily routine I functioned well in spite of headaches and intrusive thoughts and images. By contrast, in the therapy hour I dissolved into a cacophony of voices and altered states. I listened to Daddy's Girl sing "Three Pretty Girls," and I learned that she was unable to share her feelings directly with me because of the wall that divided us.

The alters seemed to know me and my life better than I did. This awareness came as a shock, but Sally observed that I was recovering parts of myself and encouraged me to let some peace come in as we wove them together.

"The process is an unfolding," she suggested, "allow it to happen naturally." I felt disconnected from and somewhat suspicious of the parts that were tumbling out, but agreed to foster a spirit of teamwork among all of us.

One hopeful dream reflected my growing trust in Sally. I went to her house, which was a large and beautiful church. I told a woman that healing services were offered there. The dream in all its simplicity mirrored my deeply felt experience, namely, that my therapy was above all a profound spiritual journey.

SPRING 1990

I'm taking care of a baby. A woman helps me.
I see the baby floating in the bathtub. When
I lift her from the water, her eyes open and her
fingers begin to move. I'm amazed that she's
alive and wrap her in a blanket.

(Dream: April 18, 1990)

One Spring evening I told Sally about a portrait at a Boston art museum, an oil painting of a Gypsy woman whose hand covered her mouth. In my frequent trips to the museum in the late seventies, I lingered before it trying to decipher the mystery of this silent woman. Only now, as we talked about my attraction to the painting, did I realize that the woman was a representation of myself, a woman with a secret who couldn't tell what she knew.

Sally said that I was doing good work in allowing myself to come apart. Big Barbie often came to therapy. "My job was to manage the inner children. When Barbara's infant daughter, Susan, died, I came out into the external world. I loved taking care of the boys, and then the girls." She reviewed good moments in the marriage: bed-time story-telling, special foods, house projects, and the beautiful flower garden she nurtured. Sally pointed out that Big Barbie protected Barbara by hiding the other alters and their memories; now her work was to let go and let Barbara know her own history.

Gradually Big Barbie promised to do her part in piecing together Barbara's fragmented life. Her work shifted. As internal parts announced themselves to Sally, more communication opened up within the system. Big Barbie facilitated this conversation while also providing a secure presence for hurt inner children.

Daddy's Girl found in Sally the attentive mother she never had. "I wanted to make Daddy happy, but what he did made me sick," she said, rubbing her body and pounding the floor. She covered her face with her hands, confused by the good Daddy who played with her and the bad Daddy who hurt her. With thick crayons she drew bold strokes of bright red rage and deep black grief. She worried about feeling angry, but Sally told her that fury was a sign of her strength. "The dirt belongs to Daddy," Sally said. "You can open yourself to the love that Barbara has for you."

Big Barbie agreed to create a safe inner room where Daddy's Girl could rest and where I could meet with her. Daddy's Girl was afraid that love would harm her, but slowly she accepted my affectionate words. She wondered if she might offer me something in return. "Could I help you enjoy your body?" she asked.

I was in awe of Daddy's Girl. Her sensual nature and strong emotions were foreign to me. I was also envious. I silently resented her intrusion into my therapy time.

A few sessions later, Sally suggested that we compose a time line to indicate when the alters emerged in my life. Sadness flooded me as I imagined these figures as part of me. "What brings you all together is your love for Baby," Sally explained. At the mention of Baby I reached for my doll, fearful that a dreadful violence would befall her.

My mind switched rapidly to my third child, Susan, who died in infancy. In a burst of insight I told Sally that I was the baby who died. "Yes," she said, having already made that connection. The discovery stunned me. "For the moment we can set this aside," she murmured.

Why haven't I known these parts of me? I searched for links between past and present. I recalled random puzzling events: sitting in a class and not remembering I had been there before; hearing people comment that I seemed like a different person; knowing that I did something but feeling that it wasn't me; feeling instability, gaps, and discontinuity in my life; experiencing an absence of any feeling; experiencing strong feelings without knowing why; hearing occasional inner voices; feeling dead inside.

Little Barbie brought her drawings to therapy. She had happy memories of playing ball on the front steps, of the warmth of her flannel-lined jeans, and of studying her catechism on the way to school. She remembered Daddy and laughed. The laughter escalated beyond her control. She rubbed her face frantically, unable to stop.

Sally took Little Barbie's hand and told her to squeeze tightly. The laughing subsided. "Daddy held my head. He put his big thing in my mouth," she whimpered and collapsed on Sally's lap. When Little Barbie receded, I felt scared and shakey. Sally soothed me, noting that there was no veil separating Little Barbie from her experiences.

At home I erupted into laughing without warning. I felt crazy. The sound disturbed Myrna. Sally suggested that I transform laughter into another sound, but it was beyond my control. She linked the laughing to anxiety and wondered if something else was stirring in me. "Pushing things down only makes them worse," she reminded me.

This task was supremely important to me because I wanted to maintain my home life and my professional work. I challenged myself by offering a paper on feminist social work at a state-wide conference. To my great relief the event came off without any interference from young alters; but I wondered what the participants would think if they knew that I had multiple personalities.

Teri joined the growing circle of alters. She was seventeen, sexy, and fun-loving; she liked slinky dresses, spiked heels, and men. Teri remembered coming out in New York and having sex with Daddy. She enjoyed sensual and sexual pleasure.

"I know some of the others inside, but they stay away from me because I like sex." Teri moved gracefully in her chair, spreading her arms and legs in free, uninhibited movements. She reported her unsuccessful efforts to get control of Barbara's life. "The others stopped me," she said. I felt embarrassed by Teri's unbounded sexuality, but Sally said that she's part of me, that she came out to spare me pain.

My drawings were dominated now by heavy black lines and multiple black circles. I called them cracks and holes. I didn't understand the markings and the terrible anxiety that fueled them.

Bewildered, I called my sister. "What can you remember about me when I was a child?"

"I feel so very sorry about the way I teased you," she answered.

I remembered her mocking laugh as she hurled Latin words at me which I couldn't understand.

"Both of us were afraid of Mom and Dad," she continued. "When you, me, and Dad were at home, he often sent me out to play or to the store. I knew he was trying to get rid of me. You developed sexually very early." I gasped. This was the last thing I would have said about myself.

Sally urged me to draw a self-portrait. The unfinished picture showed a rigid figure, arms by her side, a baby clinging to her neck while other figures hovered on her body. My heart ached when I looked at it. Sally called on Big Barbie to support and anchor me.

More laughter pervaded my therapy sessions accompanied now by images of hitting Sally. Although the images frightened me, Sally supported my anger. "We're still friends," she said. "Anger doesn't hurt our relationship."

Now I understood panic. My body felt electrically charged. The lightest stimulation was a shock. I told Sally that I couldn't connect with the abuse, that it happened to someone else. "We had best slow down; we're moving too fast," Sally warned.

Not Barbara took over. She was rigid and silent. Sally called for help. Big Barbie replied that Barbara and others inside were overwhelmed. Not-Barbara repressed all feelings. She took control when things were too chaotic. Sally suggested that I listen to this alter and identify her needs. This was a formidable task. Not Barbara suffocated me. Everything shut down - obscuring both the pain and the hope of recovery.

The emergence of Not Barbara stirred up memories of the early years following my divorce in 1975. The religious community with which I was associated requested that I leave. Some said I was a scandal; others, less harshly, felt I was confused. Their decision pained me deeply. I looked back on those early years apart from my family and saw Not Barbara grimly moving forward.

In spite of the turmoil of therapy, I completed the Master's program in Social Work. The degree brought together many of my interests: feminism, nonviolent social change, community development, and my own and others' healing and empowerment. I settled into a professional home and was welcomed by my teachers and supervisors who were aware of my psychological struggles and nonetheless supported me. Myrna, Sally, and many friends celebrated the graduation with me and I felt their benediction as two women deans placed the master's hood over my shoulders.

In late Spring, the laughter became more intense in therapy and five-year-old Jeannie emerged. She had many stories: about the kittens who died, about playing with her doll house, and blowing bubbles on the back porch. She talked about the brown metal beds. "Daddy held me down. His fingers hurt. " Jeannie covered her mouth, "Be quiet. Don't talk," she said. "Mommy says I'm bad, puts me in the closet." Laughing hysterically, Jeannie made wild gestures.

She brought a doll house to therapy, telling stories by moving tiny figures and plastic furniture. "I'll be good," she repeated compulsively. She was a lively, strong, and traumatized child.

Jeannie drew pictures of Protector, her faithful guardian angel. Protector appeared. She told Sally that she provided safety. "I prevented the little ones from talking. They would have been harmed more if they had spoken," she confessed.

I felt dazed by this tragic drama. I heard the voices of these other selves but couldn't absorb their memories or feelings. I thought about the early months in therapy when I fell into darkness and memories erupted. Were these parts giving me their experiences?

In late May, Myrna and I travelled to Guatemala to establish links with a weaving cooperative that might lead to a collaborative project with sewers in Maine. Sally reminded me to keep in balance the journey in and the journey out. I was nervous about the disruption the trip might cause, but Sally and I made plans for phone contact at mid-point. She assured me that I wouldn't lose the parts of me that I had found.

SUMMER 1990

I'm watching a film which is a kind of meditation. An image of cloth appears on the screen. It becomes increasingly dense and richly textured. A voice says, "There is only one way to be in life: open, open, open."

(Dream: June 2, 1990)

I walked along steep hills stunned by the lush greenery, abundant flowers and powerful mountains of Guatemala. I knew that the soil beneath my feet was drenched in the blood of massacres, in the ghosts of the disappeared, and in the tears and hope of those who continued to struggle. Betsy, Kelly, Myrna, and I met with members of the weavers' cooperative who showed us their fabric of brilliant threads. We agreed to a collaborative effort: we would purchase their backstrap-loomed cloth and women in Maine would create finished articles of clothing and accessories. Our hope was to promote work and economic empowerment for both Mayan and Maine women.

The profound feelings of solidarity I experienced with these weavers was strengthened by our meeting with members of GAM, the Mutual Support Group for the Appearance Alive of Our Relatives, a human rights organization formed by friends and relatives of those who had been disappeared. Sitting in their tiny office in Guatemala City, ravaged by bullet holes and bombs, we listened to Maria, Juan, and Elena tell stories of brutal persecution, violent repression, and of repeated trips to the morgue to look for loved ones. As human rights workers, they were considered enemies by the government and ready targets by the army. I felt a connection between the violence they suffered and the terror that shattered me; all inhumanity seemed to spring from the same source.

I returned from the journey better prepared to face the demons that clawed at my heels. The laughing in my head and the nightmares that haunted my dreams suggested that their numbers were legion.

When I resumed therapy, Sally and I created an internal room for Jeannie who needed comfort and safety. The peach-colored room was soft and warm, complete with plush cushions. Jeannie hated her body and associated sexual feelings with pain and terror. Frantically, she rubbed her arms and legs. "Look in the mirror," Sally suggested. "See that your body is clean and good." One morning Jeannie looked at her reflection and, shocked by her adult body, she hit her vulva, wanting to get rid of the part of herself that felt so much pain.

"His thing hurt me. I screamed but he stuffed the sheet in my mouth. I couldn't move; I couldn't make sounds," Jeannie wailed despairingly. Sally likened it to torture, to sadism.

When Sally and I processed Jeannie's memory, I felt utterly alone, unreachable. "That's the essence of abuse," Sally said. Now I understood why sheets repelled me; why I had always associated them with dirt and fear. Even when I made my bed as a child, disgust would rise in me. I never knew why.

Sally suggested that I check in with Jeannie several times a day because she seemed to be a central alter in the personality system. Counter, a newly emerged member of the internal system, made a chart and kept track of my moments with Jeannie. "I've been around for many years," Counter explained. "I like to count and that helps everyone inside feel calm."

Counter wasn't a surprise to me. I've heard her voice for many years. She confided to Sally that she counts windows, doors, lights, tiles on the floor; she counted the brown beads that Sally was wearing, and both of them chuckled.

Jeannie reported blurry vision and dizziness. Sally urged her to let go. Jeannie disappeared and No came out. No was full of rage toward Daddy and had tender solicitude for Baby. When Jeannie returned, Sally helped her to accept that No was part of her, and that she, like Barbara, was fragmented. The fact that an alter could also have alters stunned me.

Sally encouraged me to find a metaphor that would help me remain open to all parts of the system. She proposed that the holes and cracks I drew suggested a cracked egg that opened for each new personality. "Because you are healthy, the others can come out; it is a process of rebirth; I have faith that openness to pain brings healing," Sally said.

A few sessions later, fourteen-year-old Jane made her appearance. She was active in high school science fairs and liked to study. "I love exploring nature: leaves, trees, flowers, even bugs," she said excitedly.

Jane also liked to sing. For days before she emerged my head was filled with music from the forties. She suggested that everyone inside jointly compose a song. The alters put new words to "As Time Goes By" and sang it for Sally and me. The tune was a pledge of their strengths and protection. I especially liked the third verse:

"So when the journey's rough, when pain becomes too much, just turn your face to us. We'll hold you deep within our circle as time goes by. "The song repeated over and over in my mind, consoling me.

When Sally unexpectedly cancelled an appointment the next week, I fell into a depression. Did something I say or do make this happen? Once again I had to remind myself that we had a professional relationship, that I purchased her services. I was on the periphery of her life. In my sadness I despaired of the possibility of healing.

As I had done in the past, I considered not hugging Sally or allowing her to hug me. But I knew in my heart that Sally's touch made me feel protected and I wasn't willing to relinquish that sense of security. When I disclosed these feelings she was kind and understanding: "The feelings are natural because we care about each other. Of course you would feel disappointment when I cancelled our meeting."

One July evening another child alter appeared. Her hands covered her face. Her name was Shadow and she liked the dark. "I don't have a Mommy," she whispered, "but I do have a Daddy." She shook her head, "He hurt me. "

Shadow told Sally how she touched the penis of a little boy. "I wanted to see if it would get hard and big, like Daddy's. I was bad. "

"You were curious," Sally reframed. "Many girls and boys who were sexually abused also touch other children." When Shadow receded, Sally held me to control the shaking, remarking that I had gone far away. Overcome with guilt and shame, I phoned Sally later that evening and poured out my confusions. "What happened is categorically different from your father's abuse. Shadow's remorse would be helped by a ritual of healing. Create an internal room for her, with plants, light, and colorful objects. Tell her that she is good. Tell her that she is a child of God," Sally replied.

On a warm Sunday afternoon Myrna and I drove to a local fair where I saw Sally and her daughter, Betsy, who participated together in Central American solidarity efforts. I watched Sally pin a peace button on Betsy's shirt. From a distance I saw their smiles and felt the love between them.

Sally and Betsy were selling goods from El Salvador and Guatemala. The proceeds supported human rights work in those countries. When I spotted a string of brown beads like Sally's, I quickly bought them.

Sally and her daughter reminded me of the maternal love I had never had. The pain was exquisite and sharp; I had defended myself against it all of my life. During my childhood I remembered only anger and fear toward my mother. Did I long for her? Did I reach up to be held by her? When did I give up?

In therapy I wanted to wrap myself in a blanket and curl up on the floor. I felt angry, desolate and inconsolable because Sally could not fill the hole in me. "Abandonment," Sally said, "is the deepest pain. Facing the hole within yourself is healing."

In recurring dreams I searched for Sally, but she was too busy to talk to me. By day I nurtured myself in the garden with my lilies, dahlias, daisies and violets. I turned to Myrna who sat by the sea with me, watching the moonlight shimmer on the water.

I pondered my experiences with the alters. Hope presented a special challenge. A child of six, she burst into the room compulsively scratching her arm and slapping her face. Sally held her hands. "You are scratching and slapping because Daddy taught you to do it." Hope admitted that her body hurt when Daddy spread her legs. "It makes me feel better when I hurt myself," she revealed. Later that evening I inspected the scratches on my arm and worried about Hope.

Sally encouraged me to build a relationship with Hope. "She filled a need at a particular time. For now," Sally added, "just try to be comfortable with her. "

In late summer I travelled to Moosehead Lake, a pristine environment in Western Maine. En route, large rambling farmhouses rekindled memories of the summer of 1950. Jody was eleven and I was nine. My parents were separated and my mother decided to board Jody and me with an older couple in New Hampshire. They were gentle, kind people, but after one week of enduring fights between my sister and me, they asked us to leave. Undaunted, my mother and her boyfriend loaded Jody and me into the car and began the search for another home.

We drove through winding rural roads that long day, eventually locating a farm that boarded state children. A single photo of the kids who lived there captured that summer. They slept in an outside cabin, while we had a large, sunny bedroom. I saw them stand at the kitchen door at meal times with their tin pie plates in their hands, while Jody and I ate in the family dining room. I hated the way they were treated. We swam and roamed the woods with these seven ragged kids and took their picture home with us, a reminder of their friendship and of their sad, bleak lives.

When Jody and I reminiscenced about that summer, she confided that she was molested by a man in the farm family. Little Barbie told Sally that the same thing happened to her. "Inever went to the barn again," she said sadly.

I wondered why none of the alters cried about the abuse. Sally suggested that Baby held the tears. "Baby is safe now. Is everyone ready to let her cry?" she asked.

Various alters took turns rocking Baby and singing to her, but tears did not come. Instead, the feeling of falling apart - what Sally called opening up - became stronger. In dreams the earth was torn up, houses were buried in lava, others were caving in. I raced from people, trying to protect myself from assault. In all my dreams, there was danger and no escape.

AUTUMN 1990

> I see rows of children kneeling on the sidewalk
> of a city street. They are perfectly still, but
> seem to be in pain. I look closely and see that
> they are the same child.
>
> (Dream: October 2, 1990)

The roads were almost empty now of the campers, canoes and boats that signalled summer on the Down East coast. I drove slowly along the back roads to the church and my session with Sally, dazzled by the breathtaking colors of the leaves. I knew this road well: the narrow curves, steep hills, and protruding rocks. I loved especially the winding stretch along Tunk Lake whose waters mirrored the blue or gray of sky, the radiance of fall or the deep cold of winter. The lake was ever changing, promising that I, too, was being transformed. Returning from therapy I often stopped at the lake and scribbled notes in my journal. There were times I wished I could cry at this lake, wished that the water could release the tears that I couldn't find in myself. This road, the lake, the enduring rocks, the cedar, birch, spruce, and oak that witnessed to my ride, were home to me.

On my birthday Sally surprised me with a Guatemalan card and a lovely journal. She placed a thin candle on an apple-oatmeal muffin and said, "It's everyone's birthday," referring to my alters. In that moment I was both child and woman. Sally believed that my fifties would be the best decade of my life.

For the first time I read the writings of other women who experienced multiplicity. It helped me to know that others made sense of their complexity and were able to write about their voices and selves.

I asked Sally how I could not have known something so central about myself. "You're co-conscious," Sally answered. "The alters have always been part of your life but you were not aware of them. I began to glimpse them early in your therapy." She cautioned me about reading. "Don't compare yourself to others; there is a range of dissociation and labels are not helpful."

As we spoke I recalled telling Dana, a former therapist, that I felt discontinuity in my life and a sense of being divided. I remembered admitting that I felt disconnected and dead most of the time. I shared these recollections with Sally and finally grasped what I was trying so hard to say.

"Tell me about Dana," Sally urged.

A numbing suicidal depression brought me to Dana. Although I was a feminist peace activist in 1978, engaged in mobilizing anti-nuclear efforts with a wide community of friends, I was deeply depressed and haunted by thoughts of death. But therapy with Dana created its own problems.

Within two months, Dana invited me to participate in her research. We spent many hours at her home, discussing her project. Eventually I provided resources for her and also transcribed tapes as barter for continuing therapy. I didn't understand the nature of the therapeutic framework or the perplexing feelings that our relationship generated in me.

I told Dana that I felt my face was damaged and bruised. I told her about the dreams of sexual abuse by Daddy and others. Sitting on the floor by her chair, I drew pictures of being held in her lap like a tiny child. My meetings with Dana had an intense quality that puzzled me, but they eventually became a life-line. I stopped thinking about suicide.

One September evening as we walked to the store to buy bread, Dana announced that she was terminating my therapy because she wanted us to be friends and co-workers. I was both flattered and confused. Within a month, she also wanted to be my lover.

I admitted to Sally that I was excited by Dana's affection. She was beautiful and intelligent. I fantasized a bond of love between us. A few days later she suggested that we become lovers, I called to invite her to dinner. She was angry. "I resent being tyrannized in personal relationships," she shouted on the phone. "What I said to you was only a feeling, not a possibility." Pain, swift and searing, shot through me.

Going directly to her home that gray November morning, I climbed the stairs to the white porch and pressed the bell. Within seconds we faced each other in the spacious hall. "You're nothing but a prick," she screamed. "You have no right to be here and intrude on my time. You're fucking me over." She threw her pen at me. It sailed in slow motion, crashing against the oak floor. I stood transfixed, virtually unable to speak or move. Dana eventually composed herself and said that she wanted to remain friends. I agreed. Confounded by strong feelings that had no name, I left her house, my head pounding and my hands trembling.

I told Sally that I couldn't untangle myself from Dana. She called periodically to talk about her work and to ask me for research assistance, which I gave. On an April afternoon, she invited me to her bed with words of affection.

We rested in the light, airy bedroom, whose windows exposed new green leaves bursting from sun-warmed branches. I reached for her but she moved my hands, not allowing me to touch her. "I think it's sexier with clothes on," she said, curling on top of me, pushing herself against me. Finished with her pleasure, but unconcerned with mine, she turned her face toward the white wall and fell asleep. Wordless, I watched shadows move across the ceiling.

Dana and I occasionally saw one another, but I built a barrier of protection between us and gradually weaned myself from her. The pain of our relationship, especially the deep shame, remained for many years. Whenever I spoke of her the walls of my mind banged against each other.

In 1985, I read an article likening sex in the therapy relationship to incest. I began to unravel the awful abuse Dana inflicted on me. "She was incompetent and unethical," Sally said, "a bad combination. You entered therapy with Dana because the pain of your father's abuse was surfacing. I suspect the alters were active in your process. Her exploitation reenacted the original trauma."

Her words pulled experiences together from across the years, making sense of fear, helplessness, and longing. Sally asked if I wanted to take action against Dana, but I felt too unstable for that effort.

Our conversation about Dana evoked memories of other sexual relationships in which I felt submissive and fearful. "You felt that you would die when your father sexually abused you, so sexual feelings are frightening to you. They were aroused when you were little with no chance to ease into them," Sally said. She encouraged me to talk with Teri, who liked her body and enjoyed sexual pleasure, but I wasn't ready.

Within a few weeks, more alters came forward. Listener was a strong, calm presence who functioned as therapist in my professional life. "I wasn't abused by Daddy but I do know about the violence. I listen to women who were traumatized and work with them toward healing. My supervisor guides my practice."

Another alter, Barbara Davis, isolated herself in her internal room, wore earphones, and listened to classical music. She preferred to think good things about Daddy and resented talk about abuse. She remembered Daddy's death with sadness. At Sally's suggestion she walked to the ocean one clear September morning. Her hands were filled with nicotania and petunia blossoms. Releasing them to the sea, she whispered goodbye to her father.

In October a small, mute child came frequently to therapy. Sally hummed and encouraged the child to imitate her, but the alter made no sound. At Sally's urging, Daddy's Girl agreed to get a doll so that the voiceless child could show what happened to her. She discovered three dolls at a yard sale and brought them to therapy. Flushed with shame, Daddy's Girl admitted that she used to touch her dolls the way daddy touched her. Much to her relief, Sally gently said, "That's normal."

When the silent one received her doll, she hit it, covered its face and touched between its legs. She scrawled "bad" across a page in large, red letters, and drew herself hidden in a deep hole. "The hole may have saved your life, preventing you from being obliterated. It's safe to come out of the hole now," Sally invited. The child took her extended hand. "Hi, I'm Mimi."

Sally wondered if Mimi had been close to the surface in the early months of therapy when there had been many long periods of silence, punctuated by stuttering and aborted attempts at speech. I didn't know. But in that moment a pain growing in me burst out in uncontrollable, hideous, insane laughter. Sally held me and invited me to call her when I arrived home. The crisis ebbed.

Tiger and Sparkle filled more gaps in my history. Tiger was an abused little boy who wanted to kill the violent daddy who hurt him between his legs. "What he did is beyond words, beyond speech, " Sally said. Tiger wanted to hurt his own body but Sally suggested that he meet with Hope who had learned not to harm herself. Together, Tiger and Hope stomped on the pebble beach and threw stones in the cold water. Sparkle made pictures of herself playing with her dolls. "I tell my dolls secrets about Daddy and me," she whispered.

Sally rocked this child. "Imagine you are under a waterfall and all the painful feelings are being washed away," she gently murmured. Sparkle closed her eyes, drifting to safety.

After careful planning, Sally and I invited Myrna to a meeting to discuss multiplicity. "It won't be therapy," Sally said, "but an educational session for Myrna."

The three of us sat in the therapy room. Within five minutes my careful control disintegrated. I burst out laughing. My hands rubbed my face as if to erase skin itself. I heard multiple voices and I reached for Baby, rocking us back and forth. The room blurred.

From a great distance I heard Sally say that the alters were positive and helpful to me. "What would make things easier at home?" Myrna asked.

"You needn't worry so much, but if you express anger, be prepared that Barbara might retreat to a safe place," Sally answered.

Later in the day as we lingered over lunch, I felt a surprising intimacy with Myrna who had now seen me as I was. She reassured me, "It helped me to see you; I understand more now." I began to glimpse how my secrets created distance.

Sally mused, "I've only seen you that vulnerable when we were working through painful memories. " She noted that if she were to convene the meeting again, I would facilitate the process. "You may have a hard time hearing this, but I'm not perfect," she said. "I make mistakes. "

We conceded that we would likely confront hard things again, but this bump, at least, was made smooth.

WINTER 1990-1991

> I am lying on the ground. A huge flock of
> black birds peck at my body. I want to get
> away but I cannot move. I push against the
> birds but they do not budge.
>
> (Dream: January 6, 1991)

One early winter evening Big Barbie returned to therapy to resolve her great sadness at leaving the children. At Sally's suggestion, Big Barbie, Not Barbara, and I planned a ceremony of healing and forgiveness.

On the designated evening, sixteen years after we left marriage and four children, we spread pictures of David, Stephen, Claire, and Ellen on the long metal table in the therapy room. We lit a candle and invited Sally to pray with us.

> We left our children because we were afraid of hurting them.
> Sally: You are forgiven.   Us: We forgive ourselves.
> We were afraid to speak of our confusion and our fear.
> Sally: You are forgiven.   Us: We forgive ourselves.
> We were not able to face the losses our children suffered.
> Sally: You are forgiven.   Us: We forgive ourselves.

The confession of grief and hope was soothing, but not redemptive. I wanted to wind a string around myself to prevent unravelling, but Sally urged me and all the alters to be open to our feelings. "The journey is hard," she said, "but you have many strengths."

Sally also reminded me that my body was good and whole, but I couldn't absorb her words.

"Do you have sexual fantasies?" Sally asked, returning to a subject that had come up briefly in the past. The reel in my mind played on cue. I turned from her. She asked again.

I reminded her that I never touched or explored my body until my late thirties when I read a novel in which passages blended sex and violence. The scenes aroused me; I found my hand moving to my genitals.

I told Sally that over the next months in the quiet of my room I was excited by images of forced, brutal sex. I tried to banish them but they persisted. I began to recognize that I associated sexual feelings with violent acts against my body. Over the months and years I had a repetitive, obsessive fantasy, a drama requiring certain rules, compulsions, costumes, words, and behaviors. The fantasy exacerbated my feelings of self-loathing and despair. Moreover, the images and themes replicated disturbing dreams that had haunted me for many years.

Sally's listening pulled me deeper into this vortex of terror and pleasure. I wanted to leap from my chair; something terrible would happen; I should not speak; I wanted to hit my body and to punish myself for speaking what must remain unspoken. With great care, Sally said, "The fantasy is about the abuse you suffered."

Jeannie bounded out wondering how Sally knew. She laughed crazily. Her body trembled. She blurted disconnected words about Daddy, his friends in black robes, and that place she most feared.

Protector took over and expressed concern that Barbara was not ready to know these dangerous secrets. Sally assured her that she would proceed slowly, that it was safe to remember and that the inside selves could support one another.

Returning, I denied that Daddy could have been involved with a sexually violent group. I told her that the alters must be confused. I smelled terror; the alters' revelations brought death into the room.

Sally held my hand. "Your core is okay. Your soul isn't harmed. Your memories will free you from the power and control of the abuse." I desperately wanted to believe her words and grasped her extended hand.

Mary, Mimi, and Hope told Sally how they feared the scarey people, their strange clothes, the knives and the blood. Protector was tender toward these tormented children as they poured out their traumatic memories. A door to a deeply buried part of our history became unlocked.

My mind split apart in this deluge. The alters filled our drawing pad with scrawls of jagged black lines, large knives, and red splotches. Mary tried to hold her legs together but she was powerless against their strength. Hope fought against the impulse to prove she was good by cutting herself. Sally reminded everyone that no hurting was allowed.

I wanted to hide. I wanted to bury myself and the alters in silence. "You don't need to hide from me," Sally said. "The shame and dirt belong to them. They are gone. It happened a long time ago."

I was not comforted. In my daily life I startled at the slightest sound, haunted by the film of sex and violence that played repetitively in my mind. I laughed weirdly in the supermarket, but I was too distressed to care. I dreamt of black-robed men executing depraved sexual acts. In some dreams I was complicit in the abuse of others.

In a despairing place within myself I believed that speech leads to death. Thoughts of suicide returned like a rising wave. "Bonds with other women can heal the wound in you," Sally encouraged. "Other women survive; you, too, will survive." I wrote her words in my journal as if to etch them on my soul.

I turned to my sister for more clues to my history. We sat at the dining table in her small, neat apartment; a graceful lamp illumined the darkness. The television, always on, hummed in the background. Jody was wearing soft, silky clothes on her thin frame and I wore my winter uniform of wool sweater, turtleneck jersey and jeans. These differences have marked us since childhood.

For the first time Jody revealed her own fears about sex. She attributed her troubled relationships with men to our father. With remarkable openness she confided to me her life-long conviction that her only value consisted in being sexual. I listened.

Jody recalled evening trips with Daddy to the place described by the alters. "I felt lonely waiting in the car for you and Dad. I looked at the street lights shining on the trees." I felt closer to her than ever before. We sipped tea. Silence and grief filled the space between us. I was not ready to reveal what the alters were saying.

Sally saw immediately the implications of my conversation with Jody. "This is an entirely new moment. How does this influence your sense of a special relationship with your father?" I wanted to weep for my sister and me. I was furious at the endless suffering he caused us. I thought of Jody's alcoholism, her depression, and the fears that dominated her life. I thought of how I divided into multiple parts. As if sensing my thoughts Sally said, "Without the alters your life would have been damaged."

Sally initiated a discussion about ritual abuse. "Rituals heighten the abuse by connecting it to the supernatural," she said. "The perpetrators are sophisticated. They know how to entice victims, how to indoctrinate victims with beliefs of the cult, and how to make victims feel responsible for the abuse, thereby ensuring silence. Perpetrators often use drugs, torture and threats of death to attain their ends." She spoke slowly because this was sensitive and dangerous ground.

"Survivors of cult abuse often report multiplicity, anxiety, self-mutilation, and guilt. Their capacity to trust other people is harmed; their ability to see the world accurately is diminished." She paused, looking solemnly at me.

"They told us we belong to them," Hope stammered.

"They lied to you. You never belonged to them; you belong to yourselves. They tried to control your will and tried to make you believe that you were one with them."

The discussion disturbed me. I feared the emergence of dangerous alters. Sally believed that every alter would be sane, strong, and caring. She reminded me of my years in peace efforts. "Your work was a way to channel your anger about what was done to you." I began to think that the wars I protested unconsciously included the war against my own body. Sally invited us all to work with her so that such terrible abuse would never happen again.

In January the Gulf War broke out. I couldn't look at pictures of the bombing, the people fleeing in terror, the corpses, and utter destruction. I couldn't bear to see the faces of children trapped in a war zone. With others in our community, I stood outside the federal building in a vigil for peace. In the cold night air my mind moved between the public war in the Gulf and the domestic war of battering, incest and abuse in many families. I wondered if effective strides in non-violent conflict resolution could be reached if the protection of children was a primary national commitment.

Sally and I traveled to the national march in Washington, D. C. with other Mainers. We sat together on the bus sharing fruit and cheese, knitting wool socks and talking with other women about how our work might continue after the march.

The streets of the city were packed with protestors carrying signs and wearing peace buttons. We sang and chanted. Sally and I carried a banner that she and her friend Charlie had created: "Choose life so you and your children may live."

During the bus rides and march the tension between Sally and me was palpable, but I said nothing. When I returned to therapy Sally apologized. She explained that she was afraid of hurting my feelings if she separated from me. "I felt your discomfort but didn't want to leave you," I said.

"We are arrogant to think we can have an overlapping relationship," she said.

We admitted to each other that it was difficult to be direct and clear in our relationship. "It will be progress when you can get mad at me and be your own person," she said.

"But I'll be sad if you're angry and stay angry," I responded.

"We have a significant relationship; we'll work things out," she answered gently.

On February 12th, the third anniversary of our work, I gave Sally a beautiful vest of teal and blue made of hand-loomed Guatemalan cloth. Opening the gift slowly, she commented on the flowered paper and the card of two women and a child. "They resemble us and Baby," she said, smiling.

We walked to the restroom where she put the vest over her blue sweater, admiring her reflection in the mirror. "I'll think of you when I wear it."

Sally shared her image of me. "Barbara is on the surface; everyone else is underneath. This process is about letting go." She suggested that I set out a notebook for the alters to use. Within a few days there were pages of large script, block printed words and drawings of abuse.

"This is positive work," Sally said. She noted how Mimi moved between past and present; how Hope recorded her deep pain that no one in the world cared about her; how Teri was finding new ways to enjoy her body. I tried to read the pages through Sally's eyes.

As more alters revealed episodes of sadistic abuse, Sally taught us a way to cope. We learned to imagine the abuse on a distant screen and to diminish it to a vanishing point. In the process, the bonds between the alters and me grew stronger. By the end of winter, our inner team included thirty-one members.

SPRING 1991

I am a child looking at blood and bruises on my body.
My face is raw; my hair is falling out.

(Dream: April 28, 1991)

In an old journal with an entry dated March 8, 1987, I was stunned to read, "I feel like a patchwork of bits and pieces. " At the time, the feeling was inexplicable.

"We often fail to listen to ourselves and grasp our own meanings," Sally observed.

"Am I a collection of parts? Am I, the Barbara who goes to therapy, simply one of a large group?" I asked Sally.

"You're more of a process; you have the capacity to create selves," she said. "Let go of who you thought you were and there will be more room for growth. "

She drew a circle on the blackboard and filled it with tiny dots. "Each of you is a dot; the whole of you is Barbara."

I began to recognize that silencing the alters, refusing to acknowledge that their disclosures have meaning, was ultimately oppressive. I noted the irony of imposing on my selves the unjust hierarchical process which I protested in the public sphere. Like other feminists, I honored mutuality, equality, and inclusion.

Until I made the alters' experiences my own, I would be unable to let go of the past. Gradually I found an emotional space where I could listen to the multiple inner voices, believing that without each other we would never know our history. There was no turning back now.

Early in March, S emerged, moving her chair away from Sally. "Maybe you'll hurt me," she said. Sally repeated the safety rules and suggested that Protector sit next to S. With a black crayon, S drew large menacing figures. "I was afraid they would cut me," she shouted, rocking in her chair, rubbing her face and hands.

"You can let this go now; you've been carrying it around for a long time," Sally said firmly.

S frantically rubbed her forehead, trying to remove the mark of blood they placed on her. "I belong to them," she said.

"You belong to yourself," Sally said steadily. "You are your own person. "

Jeannie argued with S about telling what happened, fearing that they would be found and returned to that dark place. Hope also feared that harm would come to Sally who now knew their secrets. "They will find us," they repeated fearfully.

"The people who hurt you are probably dead. You live in a different state and Barbara is now a grown woman with many resources to help herself," Sally said encouragingly.

Many of the alters believed that an evil force had power over them. "No one has that kind of control. They lied to you; they tricked you," Sally said. "They made you believe what they said. By forcing you to do what they wanted, they made you feel responsible. Many people say and do things that they don't mean in order to be safe. You have choices now." She explained to the alters that the abusers controlled their behavior and their minds with coercion and deception. I was relieved by her clarity and understanding,

I moved in two worlds: my daily round of home and work, and therapy. I tried to keep the horror evoked in therapy confined to safe, designated times. Occasionally I failed. One morning when I was having coffee with co-workers at the health center where I worked, the anxious laughter erupted. The nurses looked at me quizzically. Embarrassed, I mumbled about an old joke and we returned to our conversation.

All of us designed safety measures to protect ourselves. The chair in my study became a haven for Hope when she felt like cutting herself. Jeannie and Mimi retreated to the porch to keep themselves in the present. S turned to Protector for internal stability. Others devoted themselves to the care of Baby. "Soothe one another," Sally instructed.

So far, my professional life flowed relatively smoothly. Listener now worked with a woman diagnosed with multiple personality. I deeply valued her courage in opening her internal system. She switched easily into altered states and many child alters came forward to tell their history. Under the careful guidance of a supervisor the work was healing for my client and for me.

At home, my preoccupations were evident. Myrna recognized the need to care for herself and she decided to take a two-month cross-country camping trip in her sabbatical year. In the evening, sitting in her gold and rust recliner, she made her packing lists, pouring over maps and marking the route she would take. I watched her, appreciating the meticulous attention she brought to all her undertakings.

She knew that this solo trip would be lonely and that her stays in occasional hostels might be uncomfortable, but her need for personal adventure triumphed. On the cool March morning of her departure we had many hugs; Myrna cuddled our cats, Cassie and Daphne, rubbing her cheek into their soft fur. She slipped into her tightly packed silver station wagon. On her dashboard were pictures of us and our home. It would be a month before we would rendezvous in Arizona.

Although I missed Myrna, I knew that this time apart was good for us. Mary and Mimi plunged into a round of drawing; Jeannie and Hope reenacted their trauma with dolls; Tiger and Sparkle played with rocks on the beach. The house became a container for their hopes and fears.

Therapy proceeded with carefully regulated guidelines to ensure safety. No one was to be hurt. The room was not to be damaged. I felt puzzled by an impulse to bring a knife to the sessions, but knew that this action would violate our contract. When Sally checked in with the alters, S disclosed that even though she was afraid of knives, she believed that she should bring one. "This is about a memory," Sally said to S.

Many alters spoke about knives. Jeannie described the big knife in the kitchen which scared her, the same knife that Daddy put on her body. Betty, Hope, S and others described their fear of the black-handled knives with long sharp blades used in rituals.

I listened to the alters and reflected on my life-long fear of knives. I remembered not wanting to touch that kitchen knife, but I didn't know why. In my adult years I used a paring knife for cutting, avoiding the larger blades. One evening when friends gathered at our house and chopped vegetables for a stir-fry, a voice shouted, "Be careful, knives are dangerous. "The women looked at me, surprised, and went on chopping.

I also made sense of other triggers that were associated with ghastly memories. I lamented my alienation from music. Myrna filled the house with a range of sounds, from symphonies to swing bands. I gravitated toward silence. I used to blame myself for not appreciating music, defining it as one more personal deficit, but it was clear to me now that I chose silence because I unconsciously connected music with trauma. The links were explained when the alters described sounds in the rituals. My sister also told me that our father listened to classical music, and that the band from our mother's restaurant practiced at night in our apartment.

In late April, I took a break from therapy to meet Myrna in Arizona. Our reunion sparkled. We sat over rice and beans, exchanging stories of life on the road and home. We hiked in the desert to admire the exquisite blossoming cacti. At night, we rested in the evening heat, glad to be together.

Back home I stood on our back porch under a burst of stars. I often paused here to enjoy the sweet sounds and smells of the Maine coast. I remembered Sally's observation that the alters shared the same hands. One morning Sally held up her hands and invited Jeannie to measure hers against them. Jeannie laughed, astonished that they were approximately the same. Alone on the porch, I was suddenly overcome with the feeling that the alters and I did have the same hands. Awe and gratitude flowed through me. What had been an abstraction was now a reality: the alters and I shared the same body. I called Sally to tell her about this moment of grace and at our next session she gave me a beautiful card depicting an African Goddess of healing.

I continued to rest on Sally's lap and on one such occasion felt held in white light. Another time, her hand resting on the crown of my head, I experienced myself as a tiny child. I was on the verge of tears. I shook. I could scarcely breathe. The comfort was so extraordinary, a radical healing. "All of you can hold hands, console one another and help each other to heal," Sally whispered.

SUMMER 1991

I'm high in the atmosphere, falling toward earth.
Although terrified, I open my eyes. A calm
comes over me when I see the beauty of the earth. I'm
not sure I'll survive the fall, but I have no
regrets about letting go.

(Dream: July 20, 1991)

I decided to attend a conference on abuse and dissociation. Sally was dubious because the majority of presenters worked from a medical model. "They don't address systems," she complained, "and the client is on the bottom of the hierarchy."

When I arrived at the hotel in Virginia I was terrified that my condition would be recognized. I listened to the lectures and heard discussion of my own symptoms; amnesia, headaches, and internal voices. Alters moved in and out. Counter warded off anxiety by noting every light in the ballroom chandeliers.

I kept to myself, taking copious notes, lingering over the book display, and visiting and revisiting the survivor art exhibit - drawings of fear, anger and hope; sculptures of fragmentation and healing; handkerchief art expressing the suffering of abused children.

Returning home I sought for ways to bring myself together. One evening I traced a human form on a large piece of newsprint. I tore pieces of bright colored paper and pasted them within the outline. The image was solid. I was many and I was one.

Sally affirmed our efforts, but knew that our oneness was merely intellectual, not emotional. The recurring fear of utter disintegration coupled with an anxiety that someone inside might be psychotic generated uncontrollable stress. Sally reminded us of her ease with disturbed people and the need to make space for all the alters.

In the first week of July, I learned that my former husband, Phil, was hospitalized in the last stages of cancer. I planned to join my children for his last days but I felt apprehensive: would the pain of the past be revived at this difficult time? Would Phil's family, whom I had not seen for almost twenty years, be uncomfortable with my presence? When Sally asked who among the alters was most affected by Phil's illness I was startled by the emergence of Jeana.

Jeana described herself as a young woman with butterfly barrettes in her hair. "I wanted to be married and have children," she said shyly. "Phil seemed nice and at first things were okay. I didn't like sex but I knew that I had to do it. Life was harder when the babies came. Phil blamed me for everything. If a baby had a rash or caught a cold, if anything went wrong in the house, he blamed me. I stayed until Susan died; after that I was out only occasionally. I feel guilty when I think about Phil; he might have had a better life if we had not married."

"You feel overly responsible, hence guilty," Sally responded. "Let go of guilt and face and feel your own powerlessness." Although Jeana took me by surprise, her presence was somehow familiar; her insights into the ways that Phil undermined her mothering felt utterly true.

I arrived in Boston on July 10 and went immediately to the suburban hospital. My sister met me outside Phil's room. "Are you ready?" she asked. I walked in. His face had a yellow tinge. The sheet was partially turned back, exposing his severely bloated legs. I spoke his name and touched his hand. He did not recognize me. David explained that he was heavily sedated.

I watched Phil, letting the years we shared move through my mind. For the first time in many years, I wasn't afraid of him. Three of our children stood next to the bed. My older daughter helped him drink; my sister tended the bedclothes. I spent the night with Jody and learned in the morning that Phil died at 4 a. m., shortly after Stephen, our younger son, arrived from California.

We gathered at the old rambling family home later in the day. Sitting around the large, rectangular kitchen table we looked at family photos, remembering both joys and tragedies. We began the sorting process.

The house was frozen in time. My old sewing cabinet, holding a few spools of thread, was thick with dust. We worked until late afternoon, transforming feelings of loss into household order. By the end of the day the children had arranged a memorial mass and made plans to scatter Phil's ashes in the ocean near his favorite fishing spot.

Sadness pursued me as I left the house. Jeana, Big Barbie, and I shared our memories and supported one another. We drove together to Susan's grave in a local Catholic cemetery. We parked the car and walked across the dry grass to the place we knew was hers.

Although we barely had known this baby, to this day we still saw her round, red face, her body slumping forward after nursing, and her stillness. We had visited her every day in the hospital, seeing tubes attached to her tiny body, and hearing updated medical reports. And then she died. Jeana,

Big Barbie, and I sat in the grass, running our hand over the place where she lay. She would always be part of us.

Jody and I went to the psychiatric hospital, now closed, where my father once worked. I wondered if this visit would help me understand the alters who talked about the cult. Protector and Big Barbie organized the alters to maintain maximum internal stability. My breath was shallow and my head pounded as we approached a small wooden structure with a porch, two entrance pillars, and small windows. I recognized it from the drawings some of the alters had done. The abandoned building, a chapel, was surrounded by high weeds. I peeked through a dirty side window and glimpsed a large, empty room. Dread overwhelmed me.

I was relieved to return to therapy. "The separation between you and the alters is diminishing," Sally said. When I described the family home, untouched by time, Sally suggested that the dusty sewing cabinet was a metaphor for my life. Parts of me were stashed away like discarded spools of thread.

I wanted to seek out information about the place that my father worked, but Sally advised, "Don't let the search for facts interfere with your feelings." She reminded me that this was a process, that she believed in my inner being, and that together we could pray to the forces of life to help us through.

A notepad left out for the alters to use was filled in a few days. Bonnie and Polly longed to be safe and held; Jenny and Sparkle were afraid that Daddy would find them. The Destroyers, three twelve-year-old boys, spewed forth vengeful fantasies about Daddy. Guardian warned us to be careful, not to tell Sally too much.

In mid-July, Myrna and I celebrated our eighth anniversary with a trip to Monhegan Island. The ferry filled with vacationers was festive. We sat close together, shielding each other from the strong wind. The island was a gem of wildflowers, gentle trails and art galleries. Warmed by the sun, we walked through the woods to the rugged cliffs. At night we stayed in the third floor of an old inn that smelled of sand and salt. The bed was lumpy, the bureau was shiny old oak. We opened the windows and let peace envelop us.

I shared memories of Monhegan with Sally. "I've sailed there many times," she responded, adding that her children have also vacationed there. At the mention of children, Big Barbie emerged wanting to tell about her visit to Susan's grave. Sally asked, "Can you release Susan so she can go where she needs to be?"

Big Barbie looked away. "I haven't let her go," she admitted sadly.

"You can keep a piece of her, " Sally offered. "You're a caring person. Your care for inside and outside children helped you survive the loss of Susan. " Big Barbie agreed.

After the session Sally described her plans to remodel her kitchen. "I'm opening the room, putting in more windows to let in more light," she said. I smiled, hearing in her words a metaphor for the work we were doing in therapy.

In late August, I had a strange dream in which my father resembled my mother, as if they were one person, and, as one, they changed into Sally. The transformation happened several times in the same dream. The dream illumined my fear of Sally and the anxiety which held me back from our usual closeness.

One evening I brought a time line to therapy on which I recorded the names of the alters, the dates they came into my life, and their experiences. We spread the paper across the floor. "Is this your history?" Sally asked.

"I know it is but I don't feel it. "

Looking at the paper I considered this complicated journey. Warily, I confessed to Sally that when I felt broken by disturbed feelings I felt close to the core of who I was.

"We have worked together for a long time, and I won't leave you," Sally said soothingly.

AUTUMN 1991

I look into a mirror and see a plastic
bag stuffed with paper. My head is gone.
I have no face.

(Dream: October 10, 1991)

I dreamt of profound rage toward my mother and woke up trembling. In therapy, I cautiously uncovered this wound, beginning with the good things my mother breathed into my life. She showed me the importance of work, the value of thoughtfulness towards friends, and the pleasure of crocheting.

Unbeknownst to her, my mother also passed on to me her own sadness, shame, and fear. I noticed how she held her head down when she walked, how she raced for a corner seat on the subway train, how she did not look at people. As a child I was aware that she held herself apart from other mothers in the neighborhood. Her only social involvement was the restaurant.

I was afraid of her, alert for her angry eyes. She spoke very little to me, and sometimes sat in a daze, staring into empty space. The moment she held the hot iron close to my face solidified her power. Her hostility and unpredictability frightened me. It was my job to clean the bathroom, to scrub toilet, sink, and tub. It had to be done perfectly. There were times I enjoyed the task, closing the door behind me, knowing that for a time there would be no interruptions. My bedroom was a different matter. She shouted about the disarray, dumping my bureau drawers on the linoleum, kicking me as I sat on the floor with my toys.

Worst of all were her mocking jokes about my chubbiness and clumsiness. Child alters quickly came forward to talk about Mommy. "I hid from her," Suzy said. "She scared me when she yelled. Will you laugh at me and hit me?" she asked Sally.

Jeannie and Hope described how Mommy put her short hair in pin curls every day and sometimes wrapped a kerchief around her head. She wore flowered house dresses, aprons, and an old black sweater in the cold apartment. When she was preparing for work, she ironed her uniform, shined her white shoes, and carefully did her nails with Dusty Rose polish. "We felt better when she got ready for work," Hope said. "It meant that she would soon leave."

Jeannie brought a large stuffed doll to therapy, calling it the Mommy Doll. It was covered in brown calico print with yellow trim. Jeannie pounded her, shouted expletives mingled with a longing for Mommy's love. She packed the doll in a bag and buried it in a closet.

Listening to the alters, a monumental sadness consumed me. Feelings of disintegration pulsed through me and I felt radically disconnected from Sally, caught in a profound despair. "These feelings are related to your mother," she said. "Your hopelessness speaks to an ancient loss, a very early loss; this is painful work. Draw, write, mother yourself; you will survive this. "

I told Sally that sometimes on Sunday afternoons, my sister and I walked thirty minutes to the restaurant where our mother worked, singing church hymns along the way. Inside the swinging door, the place smelled of tobacco, alcohol, and meat gravy. Our mother, in her black uniform and white apron, would guide us to a brown painted booth at the back of the large dining room. Her co-workers always told us how lucky we were to have such a wonderful mother.

She would bring us large strawberry shortcakes. The dessert was extravagant but I always felt guilty because I didn't like being where she worked and didn't like being near her. To pretend to enjoy the outing, when all I wanted was the shortcake, seemed wrong. I didn't like myself at those moments.

One Tuesday evening when I was about ten, my mother came into my bedroom where I sat doing my homework. She touched my shoulder and said how pretty I looked. Furious, I pulled away from her. Now, forty years later, I want to understand and heal the rage I felt.

I remember our family relaxing at a lovely pond. My sister and I played in the water; our parents sat on a blanket reading newspapers. A new awareness moved across my mind: I didn't want my mother around; I wanted my father all to myself. "He gave you attention. Despite the abuse he made you feel special. Part of you loved him," Sally responded.

I struggled with conflicting feelings. I thought I was angry because my mother didn't protect me.

"The feelings are deeper," Sally said, "and more complex."

At home, the alters continued to act out their feelings with the Mommy Doll. One morning, Suzy and Jeannie took her to the beach. "You gave us food, clothes and a place to live, but you hurt us, made fun of us, didn't hold us and love us." They shouted and pounded the doll, built a fire and threw her in. They wanted to let go of Mommy and their hope for a Mommy, but their childlike needs were stubborn.

Other child personalities entered the conversation. They described household chores, punishments, and the fights between Mommy and Daddy. "One night all of us were in the hall. I stood beside Daddy and Jody was next to Mommy," Suzy reported. "Daddy said that he pulled Mommy from the gutter; Jody and Mommy said that he was no good. I was scared. In the morning Mommy was lying on the hall couch. Her face had marks and her eyes were swollen. I didn't know what to do," Suzy confessed.

Suddenly Suzy started laughing, saying that her head hurt, and that her vision was blurred. She scratched herself, pulled her hair, and wanted to hurt her body. "Let's leave the hall," Sally urged.

"I can't; Mommy is sad. I worry about her," Suzy answered.

"Mommy can take care of her own sadness," Sally replied. Suzy laughed and held her head. "Let the feeling flow through you," Sally advised.

Hope made a cardboard knife, for her a symbol of power, and brought it to therapy. "I hated Mommy and Daddy and wanted to kill them," she confessed. She held the knife over her head and slammed it into the table. Her hands, now free, covered her face. She was almost crying. "I wish I could have loved them. I knew it was good to love, but I couldn't love them."

Sally took her hands. "How could you love them? Daddy hurt you sexually and Mommy wasn't there to help you," she said compassionately. "Shrink them down to tiny figures." Hope complied and announced that she was bigger than her parents.

Alice surprised me by her sudden appearance. She was a six-year-old who lived in Wonderland, in which nothing made sense. "I hear voices and I float," she exclaimed. "Daddy and I made houses with cards. They all fell down."

She jumped up and down on the couch. "I sat on the piano bench when mommy's friends in the band played tunes from Tin Pan Alley. I liked the music but sometimes . . . . " She curled up, covered her ears and disappeared. Sally suggested that Alice lived on a metaphorical level which might feel strange to me, even somewhat crazy. She suggested that Alice rest in an internal safe room with Protector to give her comfort.

Before our next session I wrote to Sally, expressing my belief that just as abuse occurred in relationships, that healing happens in the same way.

WINTER 1991 - 1992

My head hurts. I lift my hair and see
that my head is raw and blistered.
Worms crawl on my neck.

(Dream: December 17, 1991)

Jill, a little girl of six, emerged. She held herself stiffly, her lips tight and her fists clenched. "I had to do it. They told me."

Clinging to a pillow, Jill haltingly described sexual abuse by a group of black-robed men and her participation in the abuse of other children. "I belonged to them," she said.

"They made you think that they owned you, but it's up to you," Sally replied. "Do you want to belong to them or not?"

Jill didn't understand choice. At home she reenacted the trauma by cutting dolls, mumbling special words, spreading ketchup and burning the mutilated figures. She reported all this to Sally in a whisper.

"They aren't here," Sally said. "You're safe with me in the present. They weren't powerful; they were abusive."

"I want to hurt myself," Jill said. "I'm bad."

Sally took her hand. "You're very good. You struggle against impulses to hurt others and yourself." She encouraged Jill to draw her feelings and to talk with Jeannie. When Jill retreated, I felt a thick substance on my face, a familiar and enduring problem. But my face was clean.

After Jill's revelations Sally and I talked about ritual abuse. I wanted to run from the terrifying images of knives, blood, and bodies; from the horrible dreams and thoughts which haunted me. I wanted to escape the physical pain and psychological anguish.

I remembered episodes from my thirties. Feminist and political-religious groups sometimes invited me to lead liturgies. Honored and conflicted at the same time, I usually accepted the invitations.

"Something overtook me in those rituals." I spoke slowly, choosing my words carefully, because we've never spoken about this. "I changed physically. After the event I could recall what happened, but it was as if it had happened to someone else. Those moments disturbed me. Other people also remarked on a definite change they perceived in me."

Sally wondered if I have had similar experiences in other contexts. Public speaking came immediately to mind.

Other people frequently told me that I seemed like a different person when I gave a speech. They said that my accent, posture and facial expression changed significantly. Now, sitting in this therapy room with Sally, I began to understand the personality shifts I felt in those contexts.

Speaker came forward. She described herself as a teacher and as a major figure in a second internal system. "Most of us came into Barbara's life when she was a teen-ager. Everyone in this system has a specific function: a Priest who does ritual; a Writer who works with words; a Researcher who searches for information; an Organizer who gathers people together; and Listener who is a healer. We cooperate with each other in order to keep us functional. None of us were abused. Listener bridges the two systems and provides support for alters in the first system." I listened to Speaker and felt that her disclosure made sense of discontinuity in my experience.

Nonetheless, the alters' stories seemed like someone else's memories. In spite of my confusion, Sally was heartened. "You're getting better. I never worked with anyone for such a long period of time. I used to laugh at therapists who worked with a client for six or seven years. Now I feel differently. We're learning together."

I called my sister again to talk about our childhood. "I was so angry and so jealous of you that I threw up," she confided. "I felt abandoned. I always knew my jealousy and anger at you were connected to Dad. Sometimes I think he was crazy. I never felt like his daughter." In my mind's eye, I remembered two little girls telling jokes to each other in the twilight time before sleep. My heart ached for both of us. We decided to call our mother to arrange a conversation.

For the Solstice, Sally surprised me with a pair of purple wool socks which she knit and a beautiful card wishing me peace. She talked about the returning light and the birthday of the sun. Opening my gift to her, she smiled and held the purple and white sweater against herself. "It's beautiful," she said appreciatively.

In early January, Sally set out for a three-week stay in Guatemala. Whenever she left I felt afraid that she would not return. "We'll still be connected even though I am away. We have a substantial connection," she said reassuringly.

I distracted myself during her long absence. With Myrna and our friends I drove to a comfortable lodge at the edge of a lake. The twelve of us put together a great pot-luck dinner. We illumined the dark night with stories of our lives and the songs of women. In the morning we skied across the lake, our faces red against the winter wind. Our friendships deepened over these precious days.

In hard moments I felt that Sally didn't exist. It was easier to bear her total absence than endure the missing of her. Then, in early February, she returned. She gave me a small Guatemalan doll made by a little boy in San Antonio. She described the gentle ways of Mayan parents and the contented natures of their children. I held the cloth doll in my hand thinking of the journey it had made from the hands of a child in a tiny mountain village thousands of miles away.

King, an adolescent male, appeared next. He leapt from the chair and laughed uncontrollably. He pounded on the walls and shouted that he was bigger than they were. "I'm too strong for them to hurt me. I know that place. I know the people in black robes. I know what they did. I got away from them," he roared.

Sally managed to engage him in conversation. "Barbara is bad," he stammered. "She didn't make it stop. " Before Sally could respond, he laughed maniacally and left. I could never have imagined King and his terrifying laugh.

I began to reach out to people and organizations that might confirm the alters' reports of cult abuse. Sally encouraged me. She wondered what I knew about cults.

"I've only read a few articles," I replied. "I've deliberately avoided any professional trainings in this area." Sally identified a range of perspectives on the subject, from those who believe that cults exist in an international conspiracy, to those who cannot accept the existence of cults in the absence of solid proof.

"I'm somewhere in the middle, between the believers and the anti-cult zealots," she said. She paused. "In your heart of hearts do you believe that it happened to you?"

I certainly accepted that my father's chronic sexual abuse led to my fragmentation. But how painful and difficult to believe that he also gave me over to a dangerous cult. For the moment, I had no answer.

SPRING 1992

I go into a bus station to buy a ticket. A woman at the counter laughs uncontrollably and shouts meaningless words. She turns her face to me and I see myself.

(Dream: April 28, 1992)

I entered a psychiatric hospital, my heart beating, my hands sweaty, legs unsteady, and gave my name and my client's name to the clerk at the front desk. She gave me a badge and directed me to the elevators. On the third floor, an aide took me to a small, sun-lit office to wait for my client and her primary therapist.

The therapist, a tall graceful woman in a flowing skirt and sandals, arrived first. She told me about our client and her progress. Listener took over, her observations looming like a voice-over. I worried about the alters. Would they burst into the room? Would the therapist detect them? My terror faded when the client came into the room and Listener and the therapist gave her their attention. The hour ended and I rushed to the safety of my car.

I told Sally about this episode, about the terrible fear that I would reveal my emotional instability. She said, "I think of hospitalization as a treatment option for you. You might benefit from the socialization and group therapy. "Closing my eyes I remembered the long hallways and sterile rooms of the hospital. My body rocked back and forth; my hand rubbed my mouth. Sally watched. "All of your parts are welcome here." As if they heard her words, more alters came forward.

Karen surprised me when she talked of liking girls when she was twelve. "I had a crush on Nancy. I remember the day I brushed against her in the music room. Her breast was soft under her silky yellow blouse. I wanted to hold her hand, and touch her hair, but I didn't."

Karen recounted lively junior high escapades as a Catholic Daughter of America. "We wore green uniforms, sang 'Soldiers of Christ', and prayed to be pure in mind and heart. The best part was being with the girls," she added, laughing.

Her memories stimulated my own. I remembered a time when the Daughters were to meet at my house. I imagined how cozy we would be sitting on the red and blue plush furniture in our living room with brownies and cokes on the shiny mahogany table. The room was special, more like the parlors of my classmates.

"Stay in the den," my mother said leaving for work on the meeting day. She had left bottles of soda and plates of cookies in the kitchen, closed the living room door firmly and forbade us to enter. When the girls arrived we sat on the rumpled brown couch in the TV room. The glaring ceiling light mercilessly exposed the faded wallpaper and the linoleum floor. Tears welled in my eyes. I had lost my chance to be like everyone else.

I recalled more details of my adolescence: Carrie liked working at the drug store; Teri gravitated toward record hops. Looking at pictures of me as an adolescent, Sally said that I appeared to be a sad girl.

When Sally asked about my father leaving the family, thirteen-year-old Babs emerged. "He lied to me," she answered. "He got what he wanted. He said he loved me. He left and didn't say goodbye. He never cared. He used me." She slammed her hand on the table.

"Sometimes people need to go away," Sally responded. "He may have loved you. "

"When I got home from school that day the car was gone and the house was empty. His blue robe wasn't on the bathroom hook and his shaving gear wasn't on the shelf. I knew he was gone. "

"How did you feel?" Sally asked. "Mad. I felt alone." "I was glad he left," another voice stammered. "Daddy hurt us. His friends hurt us. They said we belonged to Satan. We didn't have to go there again after Daddy left. Do you think they can find us?" the speaker asked Sally.

"No. That was a long time ago. "

The speaker sighed, identified herself as Ella and slid back into the chair. "Terrible things happened with Daddy's friends. I tried to protect Crystal and Lea, but they were still abused and made to participate in rituals. There was no escape."

I was too ashamed to look at Sally. "You're a caring, gentle person," she said. "Nothing has changed between us." I opened my eyes and saw compassion in her strong, clear gaze.

Despite revelations by more traumatized adolescent alters, I still couldn't believe that Daddy exposed us to cult activities. But Sally believed in the emotional reality of the alters and said that we absorb things slowly, moving between doubt and acceptance.

How could I believe that my father could have hurt me in such sadistic, violent ways? If I acknowledged that the alters were real, I would have to accept their experiences. Even if their memories were not entirely accurate, they were still significant and somehow reflected my history. I vacillated between belief and rejection. "You're in process," Sally said, "always changing, never finished. Listen to all parts of yourself."

I wrapped Baby in a special blanket when I took her to therapy. The covering was a small lap-sized afghan of multi-colored granny squares. It was given to me by a group of teachers in Hiroshima in 1977.

I visited Japan as a member of an international peace delegation and met with religious and political groups. The teachers told me that they made these afghans for the hibakusha (survivors of the A-bomb). Back then, I did not know that I had survived a war against my body, but now, folding the blanket around Baby, I felt linked to the hibakusha and closer to my own truth.

"Baby is the core," Sally said. "When you were a child, alters kept coming to protect her." I held Baby tightly, sensing perpetrators of cult violence around me.

"Some alters believe they need to return to the cult. I'm afraid of them. I'm afraid of myself," I murmured.

"You belong to yourself. You're free to choose goodness. There is a world of difference between impulses and behavior," she added.

Sally urged the strong, stable alters to encircle the fearful ones and to teach them about our current life. Her words relieved me, helping me live more easily with the violent images that erupted in my mind.

Hon described his worst moment: being forced to say that he wanted to be abused. Lucy, rocking wildly in the chair, described a bizarre ritual in which a cult leader placed blood on her forehead, marking her with the sign of Satan. I sought Sally's lap and the comfort of her heartbeat.

"I'm afraid of breaking into a thousand pieces," I whispered.

"Your feelings are intense because of the trauma. You vacillate between being numb or overwhelmed with emotion. We need to desensitize the feelings and bring them down to a more normal range," Sally responded.

As the alters described their experiences in the cult I slipped into a crippling guilt. I was reminded of the Saturday night Chapter of Faults in the convent when we confessed our infractions of the Holy Rule before the community and received a penance. This ritual always alleviated my guilt.

I remembered the young nun that I was, moving on the surface of her life, confused by disturbing emotions. She mistakenly believed that giving herself to a life of prayer and service would bury the chaos and bring peace.

In May, twelve-year-old Dottie appeared. She shouted, rubbed her wrists and legs, and crawled on the floor, fearful of being seen and abducted by cult members. She had several alters, many of whom pulled at their skin and hair. Like Dottie, they were imprisoned in the past. Sally observed that Dottie and other alters who resisted the cult suffered more anxiety than those who resigned themselves.

"We need to strengthen the internal system so that Dottie and others like her who feel so distressed can be integrated," Sally said.

Listener came forward and suggested forming stronger bonds between the first and second system. "Those of us in the second system are grounded in the present and have no history of abuse," she reminded Sally. "I'm a link between the systems but perhaps someone else could help me.

Ella came forward. "I'll be a bridge," she said, "and we'll all feel stronger." Cooperation among the alters increased my confidence.

At the close of a session in May Sally announced that we had been asked to find a new meeting space. Other people who used the church had complained that I was too noisy, that the shouting, banging, and laughing interfered with other meetings.

We had been meeting in this simple Sunday School room for over four years. The space was sacred to me. It knew my secrets and witnessed my struggle. It was a place of death, of resurrection, and hope. My hand lingered on the knob as I closed the door for the last time.

SUMMER 1992

I'm walking in a building. The floor gives
way and I fall, hanging on to splinters of
wood. The room becomes darker.

(Dream: July 3, 1992)

My son David planned to be married in Germany. Myrna and I set out to find a dress suitable for me to wear. In the end, Jeana, an alter who was very active in my marriage, chose a flowered two-piece dress and black patent leather pumps; she liked dressing up.

Stephen and David, along with Tina and her parents, greeted me at the train station in Trier, Germany, with hugs and kisses. We piled into rented cars and drove to a hotel nestled in the mountains. In this old Roman city I was stirred by the blend of ancient and new architecture.

Over the next two days I met Tina's large extended family. We gathered in homes and restaurants to celebrate the young couple and to lift our glasses to the strains of German music.

Jeana, Big Barbie, and I went to the wedding. Outside the magnificent church where Tina's parents wed over thirty years ago, I watched Stephen pin a boutonniere on David. I wept. These grown men, vital and handsome in the morning light, were my sons.

Later that night when Stephen and I returned to the inn he pulled from his backpack poems he had written about his childhood. They reflected terrible emotional pain. One described daily trips to the movies to escape his father's violence. But his words of grief and fear also reflected hope and the possibility of love. My hand trembled as I held the pages.

We sat together in the narrow room looking at each other, mother and son, in a space strong enough to contain the truth of our stories. My nerves were raw. I wanted him to understand why I failed him. I told him about the dissociation, the existence of alters, the old, unconscious fear of hurting my children. He encouraged me to write to his brother and sisters because he believed that truth and revelation would help our family to heal.

The next day, David and Tina set out for Paris, while I travelled to Dachau. The camp was solemn. People in the visitors' center spoke in hushed tones. We moved quietly, reverently, through the display of large pictures. The images of skeletal forms in striped clothes depicted a grievous horror. I looked at the pink triangles, reminders that homosexuals were included in the genocide. I touched the black triangle on my bag remembering that lesbians and mental patients were among those forced to wear this symbol.

Outside I walked beside the foundations of the old barracks. An elderly nun touched the cement, other fingers moved over the beads at her waist. In the barrack that still stood I saw the hard wooden boards that served for beds and felt the desolation permeating the walls.

Passing through the gate that led to the crematorium, my steps slowed. A sadness unlike any I have ever known filled my soul. My eyes moved to the watchtowers. This kind of terror was beyond imagining.

Meditating before the memorials, I found strength in those who survived to tell the story and in those who took great risks to end this profound human agony. I left the camp grasping a picture of the Jewish memorial.

Returning home, I found that our orderly household was disrupted by carpenters who were laying a floor, installing bookcases, and doing repairs in our studies. The disturbance unsettled me. Boxes, books, chairs, and lamps were crowded in every corner of the first floor. I didn't have access to my desk, papers, or books, and felt lost without these familiar objects.

My instability reminded me of that period in my life after the divorce. Not Barbara, stoic under any circumstances, took major responsibility, managing the desperate poverty, poor living conditions, and hard work. She got us through, working in deafening factories and closing her eyes to the cockroaches that overran our rented room. For an eight-hour day she took home fourteen dollars.

Depression overtook me. My internal world was coming apart. "I'm no longer above the alters, controlling them," I told Sally.

"There are risks in this process," Sally said. "You're losing your capacity to control the disturbed alters. As you relinquish more control to the parts, you could be overwhelmed." She told all of us that "coming together is like the blending of music, the movement of a chorus into a single sound."

She brought me flowers from her garden, a bouquet of cosmos and nicotania in shades of lavender, pink and white. We said that we loved each other and she observed that it is miraculous that I can love and feel loved.

In the last days of summer Myrna and I set off for a camping trip to Prince Edward Island and Cape Breton, Nova Scotia. Our days were slow and easy. We took long walks on warm, red-sand beaches and wandered through forest trails. Child alters searched for special stones or shells. The rugged coast of sturdy rocks and mighty trees was stunning. At night we read near the campfire or relished the festive songs and dances of local people. While this beautiful outer world was nourishing, it couldn't assuage the tempest that whirled within me.

AUTUMN 1992

> I fall off a cliff into the ocean. The
> powerful water drags me out. No one can
> reach me. I am drowning.
>
> (Dream: November 6, 1992)

Deer wandered on our land. One morning a young doe stood outside our kitchen window nibbling on grass and ate the only tomato on a late-blooming plant. Myrna and I welcomed these visits as a kind of grace. But we felt less hospitable to the raccoons who, although beautiful, regularly prowled, and wrecked our bird feeder. Myrna was determined to out-maneuver them but she didn't succeed.

The animals that roamed our homeland - our two cats, red squirrels, field mice, porcupines, skunks, deer, chipmunks, and an occasional fox - gave me enormous pleasure. We moved together in one grand dance.

Sally cancelled an appointment in early September. I pulled away from her in anger. I pulled away from myself as well, denying the abuse and multiplicity. "When you separate from me, you separate from yourself," Sally said.

She was right. When she left it was as if I didn't exist.

When Sally cancelled two additional appointments, I protested, withdrew, and eventually reconciled with her. The cycle was depressingly familiar. How could I remain close enough to her for the sake of therapy, but give myself enough distance to prevent the pain of her coming and going?

I used Sally's absence to travel to Boston to visit my mother and sister. We met in my mother's second floor apartment where pictures, plants, and furnishings reflected her domestic interests. Jody was suggesting which clothes Adele might wear to a morning wedding, laying dresses and accessories all over the bed. Watching my sister and our mother from the doorway, I felt outside their circle. This was how it had always been.

At the dining table we sipped tea and talked. "Your father was impatient and moody. He liked sex more than I did. I think he had girlfriends. In the early years, he'd take his banjo and go out for the night. I never knew where," my mother said.

"He left for a time when I was about eight. Do you know why?" I asked.

"I don't know. He just packed up and left. Walter was an angry man. He'd get mad when you were sick; once he ripped up a baby dress of Jody's when she wouldn't stop crying."

"I remember when he left Norwell Street when we were teen-agers," Jody said to our mother. "You were devastated. He said some horrible things to you. He said demeaning things to me, too, degrading me because I was female."

I asked Adele about our childhood. "You were normal little girls," she replied.

"How can you say that?" Jody exploded. "The tension in the house was extreme. Barbara and I fought all the time."

My mother turned to her tea. "I don't remember."

"I want to ask you more about sex, but I'm not sure of the question," I said to my mother. We looked at each other. Silence. I was stunned by the awareness that we had sex with the same man.

Driving back to Maine I realized that we each had our own story about the family. My sister's story resembled mine. But my mother's - how could she say that things were normal? How could she not see that Jody and I avoided her, that our apartment reeked with the stench of fear, and that we were shunned by neighbors? Why didn't she recognize the depth of my silence and the confusion of my fragmentation? What did she think about my relationship with Daddy?

My mother seldom referred to her own past, and when she did, her words were few. I wondered what experiences in her childhood made it difficult, if not impossible, to mother Jody and me. I'd never know. Our mother's story belonged to her. I no longer needed her verification of my experience. As Sally urged, I had to listen to the story unfolding from within.

Dreams reminded me of what I didn't want to accept. I had nightmares about the cult, dreams of terror, coercion and torture. In therapy, I had disturbing images of leaping across the room and stabbing Sally. "They are obsessive thoughts," she said. "I know that you intend me no harm."

In late September, Sally gave me a birthday gift of dried flowers and lavender oil that she made. I placed them in my study as tangible reminders of her comfort. They anchored me, like the rosary beads in my pocket when I was a child.

But when Sally announced that she was going to the Southwest for two weeks, I was miserable. "You matter to me," she reassured me. "I'll think of you."

"No matter how much you give me, it's never enough," I confessed. Sally nodded.

In November, the results of a pap test were abnormal and I was scheduled for a colposcopy. The nurse settled me on the table, fitting my feet in the stirrups. While the doctor adjusted the speculum and began the procedure, I breathed deeply, willing myself to endure this invasive process. The searing pain broke my control. Alters cried and shouted, tears and snot spilled out. The doctor removed the instrument. "Do you always react like this?" she asked, as she turned away to speak into a recorder.

I sat on the edge of the table holding my head. A nurse steadied me. "You can rest here for a while," she offered. Grateful to be alone, I curled up on the table.

"Did you tell Myrna what happened?" Sally asked.

"Yes. She was aware of how upsetting it was."

"I think it may be time for her to join us again," Sally suggested. Involving Myrna made the abuse more real for me and I feared that it would open our relationship to more pain.

Now and again, Myrna asked me about therapy and listened carefully as I told her what I could. When I would say, "I can't talk about it anymore," she was quick to say, "that's fine." At other times, she'd ask if she was doing enough, fearing that she was inadequate in her responses to me.

Two weeks later the three of us met. I knew that Partner, an alter active in my relationship with Myrna, would also participate. I felt Partner's presence and I relaxed and put my arm across the couch behind Myrna. "We're healing. The alters are improving their teamwork; the steel door is disintegrating; we dream of a house being constructed of strong beams. The house is all of us," I said with a smile.

Sally was pleasantly surprised. "I generally don't see her so optimistic and hopeful," she told Myrna. "I guess I don't need to worry so much." I held Myrna's hand, remaining an adult, as Sally went on, "Barbara and I have a strong bond. All the alters have a relationship with me."

"The bond is intense," Myrna observed.

"It's the heart of the work," Sally replied.

On the long drive home, Myrna told me that she felt encouraged, that before tonight she wondered if therapy would ever end. I was thankful that this meeting turned out so differently from our first attempt. I took Myrna's hand, trying to hold together my daily life with the world of therapy.

In late fall, I participated in a project researching sexual abuse in the therapy relationship. I poured over the questions, dredging up my relationship with Dana. For the first time I felt a terrible anger toward her.

With Sally's help I wrote Dana a letter spelling out the ways she violated me. She wrote back, "My memory of that time is different from yours." What most disturbed me was that she took no responsibility. I didn't respond to her invitation to discuss the matter further. Expressing my outrage helped to close this wound.

WINTER 1992-1993

> I'm in a dark, cluttered basement. I don't see
> a way out. A woman opens a door high in the wall,
> lowers stairs for me, and tells me how to escape.
>
> (Dream: February 6, 1993)

Sally raised the issue of boundaries in our relationship, referring to the way I hugged her and rested on her lap. "Are you pushing me away?" I asked.

"No, I expect you to feel dependent, but I want you to find your own power," she replied.

"You had no power over Daddy. You couldn't control him," Sally said. "It's different in here. You have choices."

"The alters have been afraid of their power," Sally added. "They were frightened that parts of the system might hurt someone inside or even a person outside."

"Now that the alters are beginning to trust one another, the barriers between them are diminishing," I reflected.

When I tried to talk more to Sally about this subject another alter broke into therapy. Jamie exploded with details about the cult. After she left I felt shattered. "The cult left me in pieces," I said despairingly.

She nodded. "That was their intention."

"I feel crazy," I stammered.

"I understand your feeling, but you're not crazy. Think of the days when you were mute during our sessions - that was more crazy. Now, you are talking to me."

I was consoled by the thought that I could always spend a few days in bed if I couldn't function. Until now, that hadn't been a problem. Listener was competent and well-respected, although she worried about having some of Barbara's feelings, particularly when she worked with women who had experienced trauma.

"Those feelings are also yours," Sally told Listener. "At the end of each session, scan your feelings and tune into yourself." Listener nodded her head in agreement. At moments like this I was grateful for being multiple, for having parts capable enough to manage the requirements of work. If I hadn't fragmented, my mind might have been irretrievably broken.

In spite of the dizzying pace of the holidays I was stricken by doubt. "Am I making this up? Perhaps creating alters and a history of abuse is my sickness," I suggested to Sally.

"You're not making it up," she said. "You begin to doubt reality when something hard is emerging. Your feelings are real. You can trust them."

I showed Sally two drawings. On the first paper, the words "dirty, sick, bad" were scribbled across the page. The next sheet was covered by a black five-pointed star. "Were your feelings of being bad lessened when you drew the star?" Sally asked.

"I don't know. I draw compulsively. I don't think about it. Parts are drawing with me, I think."

"I wonder if obedient parts of you defend against painful feelings by joining with Satan," Sally mused.

"I hate those servile parts of me," I replied.

"That behavior is a defense against what really happened. If you open yourself up to all of your feelings, you'll be empowered, not enslaved," she said.

It occurred to me that the subservient behavior that had frequently characterized my interactions with authority figures, often teachers, stemmed from early trauma. I despised the fearful compliance and anxiety which had accompanied it. With authority that was remote, however, I had always been forthright and rebellious. Political demonstrations didn't intimidate me. I had never understood these opposites in myself; but now, the alters were bringing enlightenment to my confusion.

Eve and Eva told more stories about the cult. Eve was scared by the abuse, but Eva confessed that belonging to Satan kept her safe. "Do you know about the two Satans?" she asked Sally.

"I don't believe in Satan," Sally answered.

"There's a big Satan you can see and a Satan that you can't see," Eva sputtered.

"Satan doesn't exist. They tricked you. You are your own person and can decide what you want to do," Sally responded.

When Eva left I turned from Sally, ashamed. She touched my shoulder. "You need to tell Eva about the life and the values that you and the adult alters have chosen," she said.

"How can you stand me?" I asked Sally.

"You're good. You protect life," she replied.

I drove home on that snowy evening troubled by hazardous weather conditions and swirling emotions. Traffic crept. The snow blew so fiercely that I couldn't see the road or landmarks. I felt close to breaking.

I spotted an open store, quickly pulled in, and called Myrna. When she arrived, I gratefully followed her home.

On the twelfth day of Christmas we took down the tree and packed our ornaments carefully, putting away the memories they held for another year. Myrna dragged the tree down to the beach where we would burn it. Together we put the chairs back in place, vacuumed the floor, and took the bells from the door. Dismantling the holidays was as much a ritual as the original decorating. The house felt bare and renewed.

When I returned to therapy, Sally suggested that I write stories of my childhood. The child alters thought this was a great idea and raced to Writer with their memories. She transformed their anecdotes into vivid accounts of play, work, school, and friendship. I learned that I was more than the child I remembered, even more than a child who was hurt.

I was the child who liked to sled down steep hills and who liked to do somersaults in water. I learned how to do cartwheels and how to shovel enough snow to buy Christmas presents. I was the child that made May shrines in her bedroom and who liked to look at the stars. Sally listened to me read the stories; she commented that I seemed to be more spontaneous.

"I want to be even more so," I replied.

"You've tried for a long time. You needn't try anymore. Authenticity will come," she assured me.

One evening when I arrived for therapy, the door was closed. I heard Sally speaking with another client. "Give me a hug," she said. A few seconds later the door opened and a woman walked down the stairs. I slipped quickly into the office and fell on the couch.

"What's wrong?" she asked.

"I heard you ask her for a hug," I replied. "It shouldn't bother me, but it does."

"Those feelings come from a child alter who had a special, exclusive relationship with Daddy. Those feelings intrude into our relationship."

"I want to be special to you," I admitted.

"You are special to me. Other people are also special to me, just as other people are special to you."

I knew that she was right and that our relationship tapped into primitive needs and feelings which often embarrassed me.

I dreamt of Sally being in the cult. Someone wrote in the journal that Sally was dangerous and we should leave. "At times, I am your father. At other times I may be the cult. Our relationship is a reenactment of your relationship with your father, but ours isn't built on secrecy and exclusivity," she explained.

"Apart from Daddy you're the only one who knows about the alters," I said. Shocked, I covered my mouth, aware for the first time that he knew about the multiplicity.

"He called me Margie," a voice shouted. "He took me to his friends." Margie's laughter filled the room. Her tense fingers moved rapidly over her body. "They own me. They're inside me," she stammered.

"They didn't get your soul," Sally murmured.

"Daddy must've hated me." Margie grabbed her head. "I'm dizzy. The room is swirling," she said.

"Breathe. You're safe here. I won't leave you," Sally said gently, taking her hand.

I fell into depression. How could I recover? "The depression is from Margie," Sally observed. "The strength of your feelings suggest that dissociation is lessening." She took something from her bag and extended two closed fists.

"Pick one," she invited. I chose the left and discovered a sweet guardian angel pin. "You're ready for this gift. You're more than yourself," she said, referring to the alters. I pinned the angel to my sweater and wondered aloud what it would be like when all of us would be able to speak with one voice.

SPRING 1993

> I look at the ground. There are hunks of
> colored stuff around my feet. I know that
> they're pieces of me. I'm falling apart.
>
> (Dream: March 11, 1993)

One evening in therapy the air was punctured with bizarre laughter. The abuse was my fault. Why didn't I resist? Why didn't I make it stop? "I'm to blame," I told Sally.

She explained that when a child is abused by a parent, the child ascribes blame to herself. On this edifice of the false bad self, the child then creates the false good self. This leads to the child appearing good in order to cover up the belief that the self is bad. "The feeling that you're bad is a core belief about yourself," she said.

"That's true," I answered. When someone compliments me, I feel like an imposter. "

"Are you ready to give it up?"

I hesitated. "I don't know how. "

"What's left if you aren't bad?" Sally pressed me.

"I'm nothing," I whispered, surprised at my answer.

She nodded affirmingly. "What can you tell me about nothingness?"

"A void. Dissolving into a void," I mumbled. I laughed uncontrollably clutching the smooth fabric of the couch.

"Does this remind you of any religious concepts or spiritual writings?" Sally asked, calling me back to our conversation. I thought of the Sumerian Goddess Inanna and her descent into the underworld and of the Christian story of death and resurrection.

"In order to have one's life, one must experience nothingness," Sally explained. She wanted me to relate these concepts to what was going on between us, rather than to the past, but I didn't know how.

I noticed that after every session I craved something sweet. I often carried chocolate-covered graham crackers in the car to assuage my craving. This behavior disturbed me.

My mother loved sweet things. Our red bread box often held donuts, cupcakes, and other frosted desserts. She frequently sent me to the corner store to buy her a bag of penny candy: orange slices, spearmint leaves, tootsie rolls. She generally returned from her trips to Boston with chocolates piled in a plain cardboard box, marked seconds.

Although my mother teased me about my weight, she encouraged me to eat everything on my plate as well as to finish the food my sister left on her dish. "Barbie will eat anything," my mother would joke.

On summer afternoons when my mother left for work I sometimes asked for a nickel or dime for the ice-cream truck. I hated to ask; it felt wrong to need anything. She gave it to me, often with a hostile expression on her face.

When Sally and I reviewed my relationship to food, she asked whether my children had eating quirks. I called on Jeana and Big Barbie to remember with me.

"Phil loved to eat and wanted the house stocked with plenty of food. That's how he was raised. He cooked far more food than we could eat." I listened to Jeana and recalled with revulsion the pounds of sliced meat and cheese, the loaves of Italian bread, the mounds of home-made pasta drying on the dining room table.

"I wanted my children to eat in a healthy way, but I wasn't able to manage it," Big Barbie admitted. "I liked to bake; their father wanted dessert with every meal; he often took the children out for treats. This combination was disastrous for the children, all of whom developed eating problems."

"One Thanksgiving I prepared a traditional holiday meal with two pies for dessert. Phil stomped out of the house and bought three more pies for the dinner. The children's eating problems became more pronounced when I left. I can hardly bear to think of the children in those years, comforting themselves with food."

"The feeling that there's something wrong with your eating seems to weave in and out of your life," Sally commented. "We're getting down to the body. You're making progress."

I wondered if I'd ever change my ways. Over the years I had dieted, looked for a spiritual practice that might help, and daily reminded myself of the hunger and famine that most people in the world suffer. In the end I would succumb to sweet food.

As we were putting on our coats, Sally asked me to think about what gave me confidence that people could survive their suffering. "Ponder it," she said.

I thought about children growing up in refugee camps, of mothers trying to protect their children as bombs were dropping. Stories of atrocities from

Guatemala, El Salvador, and South Africa came to mind, along with evidence of increased human misery in our own country.

Was it courage that helped people survive, or hope that their pain had meaning? Was it faith in their own and others' strength? Was it that the effort to survive suffering was the only alternative to despair? Or was it that life was accepted as an unending round of death and rebirth, and hope was the foundation?

These thoughts remained with me when Sally suggested that we work toward a unified system in which the parts flowed and I was no longer in control. She reminded me that the alters had a common core of values and beliefs.

"I'd like to have a unified system for the sake of honoring the alters and all they've gone through," I responded.

"You've gone through it, too," Sally replied, touching my arm. "To stay sane, you created the illusion of control and separation, when in reality, you have neither. We'll work slowly," she added. "The process may seem like a death to you."

Sally and I agreed that the entire system would work collectively for a portion of the therapy hour. I was both eager and hesitant, tense inside and out. This was new and radically different.

The alters and I met in the internal conversation room and agreed to speak with one voice. Our union was fragile. We talked to Sally about daily things: coping with mud season and preparing the garden for Spring.

When the alters and I returned to our usual separateness, Sally said that she felt me in the system, but that the system, as a whole, was not very engaged with her.

"I feel like I'm losing my relationship with you," I murmured.

"You can help the others feel close to me," she replied. "Your gift may be the power of attachment."

She barely finished her sentence when Aura broke out. Her fists were clenched. She was loud and insistent. "My body is filthy, filled with worms," she shouted. "Shut off the light," she commanded Sally. Sally didn't budge.

"How do you know what your body is like inside? You don't have eyes in there," Sally said firmly.

"It's hurt. I want to cut it up," Aura replied. Sally encouraged her to go home, take a shower and see that her body was clean. Sally called on Ella to orient Aura to the present.

I was relieved when Aura retreated. Protector told Sally that many people inside were afraid that Aura might hurt them. "Aura is opinionated and bossy, unlike the other alters. As long as her feelings aren't dealt with, there will be internal conflict," Sally warned. She suggested that Aura be allowed to draw pictures of what happened to her.

"You built a personality system and kept Aura out because of her strong self-destructive feelings," Sally explained. "It was safe for her to come out now because there's more internal cooperation."

Aura drew hideous pictures of sexual abuse. She insisted that she wanted to hurt herself and the people who hurt her. Sally suggested that Aura work with a doll, as other alters had done. She and Sally decided on safety rules and Protector agreed to oversee the work.

One Saturday morning while Myrna was away, Aura stepped onto the back porch carrying a doll and knife in a paper bag. According to plan she took them from the bag and stabbed the doll repeatedly. Finished, she dropped the knife, held her head in her hands, and cried, "Please don't hurt me." Another voice rang out. Swearing. Swinging the knife at the doll. After ten minutes, Protector put the doll and knife back in the bag.

Back in therapy, Aura described how she stabbed the doll, but then felt sad and afraid. Aura 2 emerged, pounding the couch. "No one can take my anger away," she bellowed. "I'll cut out pieces of my body."

Sally explained that she wanted to cut out her pain, and suggested that she do more work with the doll. Aura 1 and 2 agreed. After more obsessive stabbing they finally burned the mutilated figure.

"It was awful to realize that I have those destructive feelings in me," I told Sally. She reminded me that many people have feelings that conflict with their values. The importance rested in not acting on those feelings.

I dreamt of giving birth to a dead and deformed baby.

"The damaged baby is the part of you that was abused," Sally said. I remembered that in the dream I wrapped the baby and buried her.

"Having let go of the damaged part of you, you can now embrace yourself," she said quietly. I made a baby doll and wrote on her soft cloth body: fear, grief, hopelessness. I wrapped her in a piece of blue quilt, placed her in a box, and buried her beneath a strong birch tree.

During Easter week our close friends Carolyn and Irene stayed with us. We celebrated Carolyn's fiftieth birthday with a simple ritual. The four of us gathered around a low table in our living room. Irene lit five candles, honoring each decade of Carolyn's life and Carolyn shared the joys, hopes and sorrows of her journey. The ceremony moved me deeply. Despite our closeness, I was afraid to tell them about the dangerous undercurrents that flowed in my life.

SUMMER 1993

> I run through a dark narrow maze
> trying to find a way out. The walls
> are caving in. Other people are in
> the maze, but I can't see them.
>
> (Dream: July 2, 1993)

My father died thirty-three years ago this summer. I've never visited his grave.

Myrna and I planted a crabapple tree on the west side of our house. I watched Myrna dig the hole one yard square and two feet deep. Unexpectedly, the hole flooded and we rushed to fill it with peat, manure, bone meal, and loam. The area was thick with mud and we laughed.

Our home felt sacred to us. We treasured the purple lupine, wild daisies, beach roses and dark iris that covered the land between our house and the beach. At dusk, when the sky was rose and gold, we listened to the song of the hermit thrush and waited for the fireflies to dance in the night.

Sally shared her own garden experiences. "I threw grass seed on the rich blue mud around my pond and it grew profusely. An exquisite iris also thrived," she said with a knowing smile.

I dreamt of Sally as either a gentle protector or a threatening figure. I was confused by these conflicting images.

"As a child grows, she slowly moves away from the all-embracing mother. It's necessary if the child is to grow," Sally explained. I didn't reply.

"Do you want a relationship where I provide care, or do you want a mutual relationship, like an adolescent has with her mother?" she asked.

"I'm stuck between those places," I answered.

Until you can let go of your need for a mother, you'll never be your own person," she said clearly.

"I still need a mother," I insisted, avoiding her eyes.

Your feelings are appropriate; our relationship can be both," Sally responded.

I ruminated about my previous friendships with older women. I wouldn't admit to myself that I was searching for a mother. With Charlotte, Fern, and Lynn I felt like a child. I remembered how my anger flared when Fern didn't notice me in the college cafeteria; how a friend observed that I had a dependent relationship with Charlotte; how uncomfortable I had been in my sexual relationship with Lynn, more than twenty years my senior. These feelings and behaviors unnerved me. Sally commented that "the need for a mother was coming from the child alters who were active in your life."

Just as I began to feel steady, Sally announced that she was increasing her fee. When I began therapy and during my school years, I had paid a reduced amount. Since then I had increased my payment to more adequately reflect my earnings, although Sally and I never mentioned it.

The increase she proposed was substantial. "You could either come for one extended weekly session, or two short ones," she suggested.

"I'm only a business transaction to you," I accused her.

"We have a professional relationship. I offer you a service," she replied. Of course, it was true. I paid Sally in return for therapy, but emotionally, she was the good mother whom I loved. We worked out a manageable arrangement, but the conflict broke apart the tenuous integration the alters had achieved. We no longer worked together in therapy.

As I struggled with my intense reactions to this change, I wondered if money was somehow involved in my father's abuse of me. In dreams, I found his wallet in my childhood bed. I repressed these thoughts. There were things that I didn't want to know.

Myrna prepared for a month-long meditation retreat to deepen her spiritual practice. I watched as she printed her name on bed linens and clothes. "It'll be hard for me to live with a group," she said. We laughed.

In the early years of our relationship, we often meditated together, sitting cross-legged in the morning sun. Since beginning therapy, the work of healing had consumed my spiritual energies. But I had been influenced by Myrna's meditation practice which followed the teaching of the Buddhist monk, Thich Nhat Hanh. His simple, profound writings on mindfulness, love, and peace inspired in me a deeper acceptance of myself and others.

Boy came into therapy. He was both victim and perpetrator. But he committed violent acts under coercion. "I didn't like to hurt, but I felt excited," he confessed.

I felt shame and pulled back when Sally asked for a hug. "We both need a hug to maintain our connection," she said kindly. I rose from the couch and reached for her.

When Myrna returned in July we went on a camping trip to a remote Maine lake. One afternoon, splashing cool water on my arms and legs, I noticed identical small scars at the same place on each thigh. I stared at them. Poured clear water on them. They did not wash away. My story was etched in my flesh.

I was astonished that I had never seen them before. "Selective seeing," Sally said. "The scars are real. They signal that neither you nor your alters are crazy. Are you ready to look at the rest of your body?"

The scars reminded me that decades can't obliterate what's happened or change the imprint on my body. I rubbed my thighs, trying to erase the scars.

A favorite story from the New Testament comforted me. When the risen Christ appeared to his disciples, one asked, "How do we know it's you?"

"Put your hand into my wounds," Christ said.

The powerful image of a transformed body bearing the signs of suffering helped me to accept the scars as witness to my past.

Without warning Sara 2 bounded into the room. Laughing and shouting, she lunged against invisible figures. She grabbed an imaginary knife, plunged it into the air, then pressed it against her leg.

"Did you ever see a flower blown apart by the wind?" Sara 2 asked Sally. "It's like a big explosion and nothing's left. That happened to me." She curled up on the couch withdrawing into a world of her own.

Minutes later I returned. My breath was quick and shallow. My insides trembled. I couldn't speak. Sally reminded me of the present. "Ground yourself," she instructed. I looked at the familiar objects in the room: children's drawings that were pasted on a bookcase; a doll's house that stood in one corner; blocks and toys piled on the floor against the white wall. I held myself, rocking back and forth. From a great distance I heard Sally's voice. "This is what it feels like to be sexually abused: pain, psychological confusion, overwhelming feelings of disintegration."

A few days later I picked up our journal and read these notes by the alters: Will we lose each other if we come together? (Little Barbie). Who will do the work each of us does? (Guardian) Will I die? (Mimi) How can we help each other if we join together? (Jeannie) Who will keep Baby safe? (S) Will we be able to talk to each other? (Hope) Who will be in charge? (Jeana) What if we need to talk to Sally? (Destroyers) What about our disagreements? (Teri) Will we be safe? (Daddy's Girl)

"Your questions are important," Sally said. "For now, just know that each of you will always be a part of Barbara."

In July, I received a kind letter from my mother. She wrote of her love for me at my birth and advised me to block out the past. Which was the real mother? The caring author of this letter or the volatile mother of my childhood?

"You've always had a child's duality towards your mother -- anger and hatred," Sally reminded me. "You care for your mother, otherwise, you'd just be indifferent to her."

I read the letter again. What about the alters' disclosures? Did they distort? "They had specific memories of her in specific moments in time," Sally said. "Because she is caring now does not erase the fact that she could have been abusive in the past. You'll never have the complete story."

AUTUMN 1993

> I'm in a hospital. I see a very long
> tunnel with a pinpoint of light at the
> end. If I am to get well I need to go
> into the tunnel. My body shakes.
> Someone holds my hand.
>
> (Dream: November 20, 1993)

Sara knelt next to Sally's chair showing her the pictures she had drawn: a smiling Sara, a pretty house with no Mommy and Daddy, and a tiny picture of Sara. Sally praised her. After Sara left, Sally observed that the alters were healing. "You're getting yourself back," she said.

At home, I settled into the beige chair and told Myrna that changes were occurring in me. "I feel less anxious. At times I feel especially close to you. This happens in flashes." Unexpectedly, a storm arose inside. Myrna leaned forward but I couldn't say another word.

In therapy I said, "I'm afraid of closeness. It's better to keep Myrna at a distance. I'm afraid of sexual feelings toward her." The pounding in my head blocked out feelings.

Sister made her presence known. "Sex is bad and we shouldn't talk about it." She crouched forward, her voice low and intense. "It's bad to talk about bodies," she warned.

"Sex is good. I like it," Sally responded. "Why don't you and other alters write out your feelings about sex. Perhaps you could agree to disagree."

I had a name for my distress - The Sleeping Giant. She was waking, stirring up sexual feelings. I paced the floor in the moonlight, laughing in that weird way. My head ached; I didn't want sexual feelings. They meant violence and shame. "Openness to all parts of yourself brings healing," Sally commented wisely.

One early morning I sat on our pebble beach watching the eiders and black ducks in the bay. For a moment I saw myself clearly: distressed and fragmented.

"What did the experience feel like?" Sally queried.

"I was frightened by how disturbed I am," I replied.

"You have a deeper acceptance of who you are. You transcended your separateness," Sally observed.

Perhaps.

Pat, a friend and colleague with whom I shares the same birthday, suggested that we plan a party. Our years together formed an even hundred. We invited our friends to celebrate a centennial birthday sock hop. Everyone in our circle came. We rolled up the braided rug and danced into the night. Times like that reminded me that there was more to my life than therapy.

I noticed new themes in my dreams. Sometimes I was both the hurt child and the child observing the abuse. In other dreams I looked into a mirror at a face I couldn't recognize. Or I was an adult in child's clothing. In a few dreams I was invisible, wandering like Alice in Wonderland in a world where objects changed size. In one, I was in a group of people struggling to say the same thing, but we couldn't speak.

"You're dreaming of your own dissociative process," Sally said. "It's a sign of progress and perhaps an indication that the little ones are growing up."

We returned again to the challenge of talking. In light of the current right-wing backlash which blamed therapists for implanting memories of sexual abuse, Sally believed that it was imperative for survivors to speak. She encouraged me to let go of my preoccupation with other people's opinions.

"Shame has kept you silent. Separate your revelations from the reactions of others. Some may believe you, others may doubt. It takes time for people to absorb the reality of child abuse," she advised.

I silently wondered if I would ever find my own words.

I stumbled into another painful cycle. "What would you lose if you gave up the pain?" Sally asked.

"I would lose our relationship," I answered.

"That would be a significant loss," Sally said. "I wonder if pain is your way of being close to people."

What was she saying? "I don't like pain. I want it to go away. I want to feel pleasure," I finally stammered.

"You've never developed that part of yourself, but other parts have that capacity," she responded.

My vision blurred. I picked up my things. "You don't want to listen to me," I shouted, leaving the room.

"That's not what I meant," she said, her words trailing after me.

I felt dreadful about my behavior and called Sally three days later to apologize. She acknowledged that she missed the boat, that she thought I was in a different place.

We decided to identify my goals in therapy. I listed integration, ease with my body, diminishment of anxiety and headaches, learning to talk about my history, and experiencing one consistent, continuous reality. Sally reminded me of the gains I had made in some of these areas, and she posed a question: "Can we work on integration with the whole system?"

I remembered our earlier unsuccessful experiment. I was the only one in the system consistently striving for integration. I wasn't even sure what some alters felt or thought.

"I'm not sure how your process works. I'm trying to understand. Integration is more complex than we in the field formerly grasped," Sally said. We agreed to repeat our previous attempt to have the entire system come to therapy for the next four weeks.

Sally reminded us that there was no one right way to proceed, that she had no expectations.

"Sometimes I fear that you won't like integration. You're used to control and internal order. This will change," she said slowly.

"I want to feel whole and stable," I responded. I took to heart the goals we had outlined. At the next feminist social work meeting, focused on secrets in our work life, I told the group that I had a history of abuse and a dissociative disorder. The group fell silent. One woman suggested that to reveal my problems at work might alarm the employer. Another woman believed that at professional conferences the more one told about her personal life, the less seriously she was taken. A third woman quipped, "What a neat secret." I looked down at my folder, feeling oceans away from my colleagues.

WINTER 1993-1994

A woman holds my mouth open and places
a tube inside. Liquid squirts into my
mouth. I gag. I cannot breathe.

(Dream: February 24, 1994)

Nicky drew sharp red lines showing the abuse she suffered. She worked rapidly making large pictures on oversized newsprint. Sally placed her arm around her. "I like you. I'm sorry that happened to you."

"No one ever said that to me," Nicky replied. Sally wondered who came out to help Nicky. Ella appeared. "There was nothing we could do but resign ourselves. We supported each other inside when we could and came out to relieve each other when things were hard," Ella explained.

Sally listened. "People have different responses to pain," she said. "Nicky responds with anger; you respond with sadness and resignation. The system always resonates when new alters appear but after they process their experiences and feelings with me it is more tranquil," Sally said. "With every new alter my perception is confirmed that your core is okay."

I closed my eyes and breathed.

Early the next morning, I sat at the kitchen table watching the squirrels scratch for seeds under the snow. The chickadees swooped to the feeder on this cold bright morning. Daphne, our gray and white cat, watched stealthily from the nearby step. Contemplating this circle of life, it occurred to me that each of the alters had a piece of my history; no one of us had the whole story. This was no longer just an idea, but an emotional truth.

I remembered how startled I felt when Sally explained that Listener was a grown up version of Jeannie; that Hope was a younger version of Jane; that Protector was an older rendering of Shadow. I experienced them as distinct presences, but I also knew that there was one body and hence, one life.

"I'd like to check in with Listener," Sally requested at our next meeting.

"Work is more of a challenge. Anxious feelings are seeping into me. When women disclose their painful feelings I feel them more deeply," Listener said wearily.

"Let's back up. Perhaps working together is premature. You'll come together when you're ready," Sally suggested. "It's not wise to release more snakes than we can handle."

"Good. Letting down the walls is disruptive," Listener agreed. Sally was concerned about Listener's vulnerability. She invited Big Barbie, Guardian, and Protector to shield Listener from the alters' feelings. Walls were put back in place and increased stability returned.

"I respect Listener and the work she does very much. Being both a client and a provider of services is hard. The secret must weigh on you."

"Yes. I move in each world, but never feel complete in either one," I responded sadly.

I wrote to a dozen organizations to get information about cult activity in Boston between 1945 and 1953. Sally wondered what part of me wanted to do that. "There's a group that wants the material," I answered.

"Other parts might be afraid that someone wants to return them to the cult," she suggested. "The group that wanted you to write is brave; it wants to face the fear head on. Other parts aren't ready for it," she explained.

Peril suggested a meeting of the alters who identified themselves as either defenders, stabilizers or protectors. "There are about fifteen of us," she added. "We could take turns staying in the center room." Peril believed that these alters would promote internal stability. Sally applauded the plan and the increased security benefitted the alters.

I came across an article about false memories and the implausibility of dissociation and repressed trauma. I already suffered from considerable self-doubt. "The words touch something vulnerable in me, the part that doesn't want to believe what happened is real," I told Sally.

"When you began therapy you believed that your father was good and that he was absent for most of your childhood. You've learned that he lived with you for over ten years and that he sexually abused you. Your sister has corroborating experiences. This is a clear case of dissociated memories," she reflected.

As if reading my mind and sensing my fear about yet another obstacle to speaking, Sally gently said, "Someday you'll be able to talk about your experiences without fear."

"But I'm not always sure that my experiences are real," I replied.

"The abuse is real. The alters are real. Your doubts stem from dissociation," she added.

Sally's forthcoming vacation, scheduled between February 10th and March 22nd, dominated my mind. I was obsessed with her leaving. I threw myself into the holidays, knitting purple socks for my friends, trying to dull my grief with the soft wool that moved through my fingers.

She'd travel first to Chiapas, Mexico, the scene of the recent Zappatista uprising, and then to Guatemala to support the refugess who had returned to their land. I worried, but she promised that she would remain safe.

On the first day of the new year I thought about how the world had changed in the past six years since my therapy began: dramatic changes in the Soviet Union, war in the Persian Gulf, the collapse of the Berlin Wall, the war in Bosnia, increased racism and poverty in America, and an expanding awareness of environmental destruction. My own fragmentation seemed like a microcosm of these external events. In the past I would have closely followed the unfolding of these historical moments, but now I struggled to hold myself together.

As alters exposed more of the atrocities of the cult, I was terrified that a dangerous alter would emerge.

"Do other people have parts of themselves that they're afraid of?" I asked Sally.

"Yes, and they try to keep down those parts by any means," she answered.

One mid-January evening Hope talked about her fear of Mommy. I carried Hope's fear with me when she receded. "Remember that you're big now," Sally advised.

"You're tall like my mother," I said.

"Stand up," Sally urged.

We stood back to back in the center of the room.

"I'm only five feet six inches," Sally said.

I was stunned. "I thought you were taller than me!"

Sally was astonished. "Many parts of you are locked in the past. We need to find a way for you to have an accurate sense of your size in the present."

Sally's departure date was now only a few weeks away. She knew that her leaving was hard for me. It was hard for her, too. "I'll miss you and our time together," she said.

"In the past I was never sure that people would return," I said. She assured me that she would come back. I asked her to make a tape for me to listen to while she was away.

"What a good idea," she said in agreement.

After our meeting I sat in my car sipping cold coffee. To know that I could hear Sally's voice while she was away gave me some solace; nonetheless, I despaired.

Alters came forward at our next session. Not Barbara was remote and cool toward Sally. Jeannie was bereft; she still wanted Sally to be her Mommy.

Myrna was worried. She had never seen me in such an extreme state.

I told Sally that I wouldn't let her close to me again. "I made a mistake. When we had a problem I always let you come close because I felt sorry for you." I recognized that I created a barrier between me and Sally as I did with my own mother. I also felt pity for her which was characteristic of my relationship to Daddy.

"Maybe you can resolve the feelings differently this time," Sally replied.

She explained that we were talking about rapprochement, a stage of development that occurred around two years of age. "Mother leaves and the child is able to retain a connection with her while she is away."

"I don't want a connection with you. I need to let go of you. You'll only hurt me again," I stammered angrily.

"You feel powerless," she observed. I nodded. I dreamt of killing Sally and linked the painful feelings to my father. "He said he could do anything he wanted to me. I'm dissolving. I've no skin," I mumbled.

"Breathe," Sally said calmly. "Come into the present." I got up, paced the floor, and wrung my hands. For the past several days voices in my head had expressed anger at Daddy for leaving after all they did for him. I collapsed on the couch.

I suffered through this arduous process and slowly gained a new perspective; Sally became a separate person with whom I could still feel connected.

We said a warm goodbye in the frigid February night air.

SPRING 1994

> I'm riding on a fast-moving train. The train
> crashes through a wall and slams against another
> wall. I'm bruised, cut and bleeding.
>
> (Dream: March 29, 1994)

While Sally was away I flew west to visit my sons. Stephen took me on my first kayaking adventure on the back bay of Newport Beach in Southern California. We glided peacefully in the still water, comfortable with each other, enjoying both talk and silence. Later in the day I had a luxurious facial massage he had arranged for me in the sports facility where he worked; in the evening we discussed writers and books while browsing in his favorite bookstore in Laguna Beach, a haven for lesbians and gay men. He knew I'd like it!

David and I drove to Death Valley. The landscape was stark. Here and there sprigs of green poked through the dry surface of the land. An uneasy silence of words not yet spoken hovered between us. I invited him to let me know when he was ready to talk about the pain he suffered as a child.

I waited for Sally's return, listening to the tape over and over. At the end of it she said, "Take a walk on the beach for me, will you? I'll be on the beaches in Mexico and you live on a beautiful beach, too. Hear the birds in the trees. Feel the surf on your face. Know that I'm not far. Love you. See you in the Springtime, Sally."

On March 23rd, I eagerly climbed the stairs to her office. She was standing in the center of the room.

"Welcome home," I said. We hugged.

"My trip was terrific. I formed permanent friendships in the cultural center where I lived in Guatemala. I'll be going back to work there."

My heart sank. She took a beautiful handpainted bookmark from her bag and gave it to me. "I hope you like this. I thought of you many times while I was away." My fingers traced the yellow flowers on the stiff brown paper. I slid onto the couch. Sally was going away again.

"Catch me up on what you've been doing," she urged.

"I'm afraid to begin our work. I need to break my attachment to you."

"Our work is important to me. I'll be going away again, but I want to be with you now and continue the work," Sally answered softly.

She sat in the gray striped chair smiling at me. I couldn't ask more of her than she was willing to give. Letting go of my fear and sadness, I reviewed the past six weeks.

I was especially pleased to tell her about the work of our local child abuse prevention group. In addition to our annual work of distributing buttons and writing newspaper articles to promote safety for children, we also exhibited art created by women who were abused as children. She nodded approvingly when I told her that I came out as a survivor in our organizing group and contributed a piece to the exhibit.

I avoided talking about traumatic dreams and internal confusion, about the voices of child alters that I hear in my head. "I'm still afraid of them and their pain," I confessed to her.

"When you shut down to the young alters' pain, you also shut down to those who have strengths," Sally reminded me.

I relented. Alters emerged to tell their stories. "They have done their part in revealing their memories. Now they can go away," Sally explained. I was puzzled. She seemed to be rushing me.

She encouraged me to draw the system and figure out relationships among the alters. The assignment frightened me. I wasn't sure that I grasped the structure of the system and I feared Sally's criticisms. But with the help of the alters I created a map of all of us and showed it to Sally at the next session.

"This isn't what I had in mind. You cluster alters according to their feelings," she responded. I hid my paper back in the brown envelope.

At the next session she showed me her drawing which identified core adults, points of conflict, children who were currently active, and alters with specific roles. I was intrigued by the center line that linked Big Barbie, Jane, and Jeannie. "They are versions of each other," Sally pointed out. I pondered her words, but I couldn't quite grasp her meaning.

One early April evening Sally announced that she would be leaving in a week to participate in a Maine delegation to El Salvador to monitor elections. I tried to respond generously.

"Will you take me in spirit?" I asked.

She hugged me. "Why don't you come. The only problem is getting a visa."

We walked down the stairs talking about the trip. I had been involved in political support for the people of El Salvador since 1978 but I never visited the country. This trip seemed like a special opportunity. Myrna encouraged me to go.

On the phone later that evening Sally provided more information. Within twenty-four hours everything was in place. I wanted to be honest with myself. Was I going only because of Sally? I wanted to travel to Central America with her, but I also knew that solidarity work was a high priority for me. If someone else had invited me would I be just as eager?

"I want to minimize our interactions while we are there so it won't be like the trip to Washington," I said.

"We'll both be part of the Maine delegation. It'll be intense, close work," she replied.

"Perhaps I shouldn't go," I responded curtly.

"We're only exploring the question. There's no need to rush to a decision. The experience would be helpful for those parts of you that connect with suffering people. Most therapists would never consider this, but I respect you and your strengths."

I felt her ambivalence but said nothing. Over the next few days I thought and dreamt about the trip.

Sally called to request an emergency meeting on Sunday morning. Seeing my anxiety, Myrna drove me to the appointment and waited for me at a nearby restaurant.

Sally seemed unusually tense and sat forward in the chair. "I've been muddled," she said. "I felt your enthusiasm and that got in the way. This is the biggest blunder I've made with you. I can't handle your going. It would be unethical."

I couldn't absorb her apology or her admission of responsibility. All I heard was her rejection.

"I don't trust you. You invited me to go," reproaches tumbled forth furiously.

"I don't remember that," she said.

"As we were leaving you asked, 'Why don't you come?' Later, on the phone, you gave me more information," I retorted.

"It was a casual invitation. I didn't mean it seriously. When you called I should have expressed my doubts."

I left the room in silence.

Not Barbara took over at the next session. She closed herself inside a walled space where no one could reach her. Sally listed all the overlaps we had : professional groups, political work, teaching at the same school, enjoying the same concerts.

"We've talked about things far beyond therapy: my family, conferences, books. I think these things have hurt us," she said firmly. "Are you willing to work this out?"

Not Barbara broke her silence. "I don't want you to hurt us again. You're like Mommy and Daddy. You hurt us and leave us."

Sally fidgeted in her chair. "It's good that you can be angry at me. Is there anything I could say or do that would help?" Not Barbara was silent.

Myrna was furious at Sally. "She should have thought it out," she said, slapping her hand on the kitchen counter. Her anger validated my own.

Our friends, Barbara and Marlene, met us for a picnic at Camden Park. "It never should have happened," Barbara said. "That must have been terrible for you."

Marlene sat facing me across the picnic table. "Sally had a problem with boundaries; it wasn't your fault," she said thoughtfully. I knew that Myrna and our friends were trying to help, but I felt hollow.

I had been disappointed by other people, but Sally was more than herself; she was my mother and father. Given the powerful transference, our relationship was as much about them as it was about her.

Sally left two days later. I dreamt of mutilated bodies with their mouths open.

She returned in ten days. Sally talked about the delegation, but I didn't want to hear it. I resisted her smile and her efforts to reach me.

"What does this disconnection from me give you?" she asked.

"I don't feel safe being open with you," I replied.

"You need to be open to yourself. How is it that you're not open to your strong adult parts that could help you with this?"

At home I listed my complex feelings:

1. I tried to internalize Sally's rational explanation for what happened. It was a simple mistake for which she apologized.
2. I wanted to remember that Sally once said that she would never hurt me intentionally.
3. I felt that she was repulsed by me and rejected me.
4. I wanted to believe that she was shaping a therapeutic process that would be healing for me.
5. She forgot that she had invited me. I felt that I didn't matter to her.
6. I didn't feel safe with Sally. This was a substantial loss.
7. The conversation about the trip took place after the therapy hour. Her commitment to me ended at the close of the session.
8. I felt that she enjoyed watching me suffer. I didn't want to believe that this was true.

9. I was angry at myself for not taking seriously the early ambivalence she expressed.

10. I felt that Sally was laughing at me.

She read the list slowly and attentively. "I've tried to diminish your suffering. I'm not laughing at you." She placed the list on a table and looked thoughtfully at me. "I was disappointed that you couldn't go on the trip. At first I thought it would be good for us, but I had second thoughts. We need to be sure this doesn't happen again. Feelings of rejection happen when there are expectations. We have an intense relationship."

Frozen with rage at the far end of the couch, I heard Sally urge me to understand that my anger toward her was healthy. She again wondered why I wouldn't elicit help from adult alters.

"You're stuck in the child system," she said. "You need the adults to help you clarify. If you open to your whole system, our relationship will be stronger."

Unable to forgive Sally, I turned to the alters. Big Barbie and Protector reminded me that this was just a moment in a process. Hope showed me her healthy arms, freed of cuts, thanks to Sally's help. Jeannie, eager to please Sally, left a pot of sunflower seedlings on her car. With this help from the alters I began to thaw.

The shame I felt for my behavior toward Sally now outweighed the rejection I felt earlier.

"There's a lesson here," Sally observed. "Perhaps your old way of controlling pain isn't helpful. I felt a certain impotence. I missed you. I couldn't help someone who was closed to being helped."

Despite my sincere apologies, I worried that my anger had pushed Sally away. She admitted that our relationship wasn't glorious, but neither was it irreversibly harmed. "I felt intensely connected to you during this process," she added.

"I felt no connection with you and no connection with myself," I replied. "I wonder if there's something else wrong with me in addition to MPD?"

Sally replied that I did have another disorder linked to my role in the personality system. "If one suspects that there's a ghost under the bed, better turn on the light and see what's there," she quipped.

"Some of your parts have done things of which you disapprove. Because of this you feel that there's something terribly wrong with you. Your feelings are directly related to your fear of the alters and to your rejection of their behavior."

Sally asked Listener to consult the diagnostic manual and work out a diagnosis for Barbara. Listener made a list of my symptoms, particularly as they appeared in my relationship with Sally: anxiety, mistrust, fear of anger, outbursts of anger, impulsivity, withdrawal, dissociation, discontinuity, idealization, dichotomous thinking, and fear of abandonment. At the next session she asked Sally if the diagnosis was borderline personality disorder.

"Yes. Barbara's disappointment about the trip led to an outburst of anger that was difficult to resolve. Barbara has specific traits that are borderline; she doesn't have a borderline condition."

I listened, perplexed and shamed by Sally's assessment. We sat silently for a few moments before Sally spoke. "I think that to work toward integration we need a new contract that gives all the alters equal responsibility for therapy and equal opportunity to come out. I'm here for you and will help you reach your goals," she added gently.

Sadly, I accepted the shift, recognizing that it was a turning point. As we walked into the May evening Sally said that she was going away for another week. I checked my calendar at home and discovered that of forty-two possible meeting times since the beginning of the year, Sally and I have had only nineteen sessions.

SUMMER 1994

I'm walking on a city street lined with
huge bombs. I'm frightened. They could
explode at any time.

(Dream: July 3, 1994)

We began the summer by setting specific goals: integration; being in the present; reducing anxiety, shame, and fear; and developing the ability to express anger directly. I was determined to work hard as a member of the system, in part to compensate for the recent blows to my relationship with Sally. I wished I could take back the hurtful words and the angry silences.

All of us joined together in therapy, but the union was fragile. "We're scared and tentative but willing to try," we confessed.

We described two painful dreams. In the first dream a woman was locked outside a building because she was crazy. When the people inside let her in, she raced into the building scratching her face and arms. In the second dream a woman was telling a group the story of her life. No one listened. She raised her voice and gestured wildly. Again, no one listened. She fell silent.

"The dreams are about differing points of view in your system," Sally offered. She encouraged me to meet with alters in the internal conversation room to explore our perspectives on the subject of talking about the trauma.

We followed her recommendation and learned that some members believed it was beneficial to talk in appropriate situations; others believed that something disastrous would happen if they talked under any circumstances; some thought that silence would keep the abuse buried; a few wanted to talk to anyone who would listen. Our divisions on this subject were sharp and clear.

On the second Saturday in June, I joined with a few friends to help a colleague prepare for her move across the country. Amidst sorting and packing I heard the words that shattered my world, "Did you hear that Sally was diagnosed with lung cancer?" Papers fell from my hand. I slowly picked them up, avoiding the eyes of my friends.

Laura continued. "Not much is known. She'll be going through tests to determine the prognosis and course of treatment."

I moved into a dark silent inner world. Although these women were my friends and Sally's, they didn't know that she was my therapist. I continued to sort and pack, but my talking ended and my grieving began.

I told Myrna the news. I fell into our bed and she held me tenderly.

I thought of nothing but Sally's illness. At work I checked the medical texts for information, but I didn't know enough about Sally's cancer. I gathered gifts for her healing: a piece of rose quartz, a labrys pin, and a tape of soothing women's music. I placed them in a small, brightly colored Guatemalan bag. I took the bag along with a bouquet of purple, rose, and white flowers to our meeting.

Sally welcomed me with a hug when I arrived. She accepted the flowers, but turned away from me.

I sat on the edge of the couch nearest her chair. "How have you been feeling?" she asked.

"I know about your illness."

"I planned to tell you tonight. We need to end our work," she said, looking at the floor. Try as I might, I couldn't hold back my tears.

"I have a tumor on the top of my left lung. I need more tests. The future is uncertain." Her skin was sallow. She rubbed her chest where the tumor grew. Fear seized me.

"I can't process the termination with you; it's too big. I'm referring you to another therapist. It's all arranged." She coughed, wiped her mouth, and reached for a glass of water.

My tears spilled over. "I'm depleted. I can't deal with your sadness," she confessed.

I mustered all my strength to contain the tears. "I love you, Sally. You've done all you could to help me. We learned so much from you. Can you say anything about the work we shared?"

"I've said everything that I can say. I'm spent. There's nothing left."

"I want you to heal," I protested.

"I may not heal. This may be terminal. I can't look ahead. I don't want to give you or me any false hope," she said solemnly.

I tried to absorb the shock. I longed to make the cancer disappear. I glanced at the clock to count the minutes I had left with her. The ground was slipping away from me.

"I'll pray for you, Sally." I sat on the floor beside her chair and placed my small gifts on her lap. She held them gently and thanked me.

I was overwhelmed by so much I wanted to say. I returned to the couch. "I love your faith and your strong love for life, but never a hoarding of it," I told her.

"Even if that's true in only a small way I appreciate your words," she said.

My thoughts raced back through the years. I reminded her of the dream in which I washed her feet. "We've had some special moments," she said quietly.

"I'm sorry about my anger toward you," I said, remembering my icy withdrawal from her.

"I forgive you. Can you forgive yourself? Learn from what happened," she added.

I listened carefully to each word wanting to remember every syllable. The minutes were dwindling away. I felt so close to her and so far away.

"You have done a lot of healing," she said, looking at me intently.

"You have given me some of your own spirit," I replied.

"Sometimes that happens," she said with a weak smile.

The room filled with shadows. I memorized her in this moment. Her thick gray hair, her rose sweater and gray slacks, her steady blue eyes, and the way her hand rubbed her chest as if to wipe away the tumor. Our time together came to an end.

We stood together in the room for the last time, hugging one another. "Take this hug with you. I love you. You're precious to me," I managed to say.

"Those are my feelings exactly," she said, pulling away from me.

We walked down the stairs and I slipped my arm through hers knowing that we'd never do this again. We paused for a hug. I took in her strong, lined face, the warmth of her arms. My fingers touched her cheek. "I love you."

"Love you," she said as we moved toward separate cars. I drove. My body shook with wailing. Myrna opened her arms to me and helped me to bed.

In the morning I decided to call Shirley, the therapist Sally recommended. Knowing that Shirley had been Sally's consultant eased the transition. She agreed to meet me the next day.

Tears streamed down my face. I couldn't bear the thought of going to work. Instead, I reached for the yards of Guatemalan cloth I bought earlier in the year. I had planned to make a quilt for Sally when therapy ended. I never imagined that the end would come so soon or so brutally.

The cloth soothed me and sustained my connection to her. Brilliant colors - red, purple, blue, and gold- spoke to me of hope and courage. I cut, pieced, and sewed. The patching together symbolized the journey of healing. I imagined her warmed by the quilt and comforted by the love with which it was made. I stitched my hope for her into the cloth.

Shirley and Sally shared an office. I felt dazed returning to this place. I drowned in an outpouring of voices and a sea of tears. Words about Sally filled the room -what she said, how she held us, her cancer, our regret that we were angry.

Shirley sat in Sally's chair. I didn't look at her. I heard her say that she would consult with Sally. "You're grieving, doing what you need to do," she said quietly.

I walked on our beach and thought of Sally's love for the water and her passion for sailing. A shining seal crawled onto a nearby rock. How Sally would have enjoyed that sight. The early summer flowers, too, reminded me of her. I wrote letters to her that I didn't mail.

Friends told me that Sally's condition was serious. The cancer had metastasized, one lung had collapsed. I was relieved to learn that she was surrounded by her children and her friends.

In therapy I plunged into chaotic ramblings. I couldn't stop the flood of tears and voices. I wondered if I was dying - perhaps I should put my affairs in order. Voices spoke of regrets, issues that weren't resolved, and hugs that were withheld in anger. Did Sally become sick because of the terrible violence that we disclosed?

I sat with my back to Shirley. My eyes were closed. "You wonder if your relationship with Sally was real," I heard Shirley say. I wondered how she knew this.

I told Shirley how I made Baby and brought her to therapy. "I was afraid of Sally but I believed that we could work things out between us," I stammered. Voices talked about the good Sally and the harsh Sally. I wondered if Sally was relieved to be free of me. I couldn't stop the outpouring of words and the stream of tears.

"I'm going to take care of myself," Shirley said at the close of our second meeting. Her words fell into a deep place in me. She would protect her health. Although she had said very little so far, I heard her sighs and sensed her listening ear.

In late June I finished the quilt, tied it with a soft blue ribbon and sent it to Sally. I let her know that I would be travelling to Guatemala in the summer with a delegation of Peace Brigades International. We'd be on a mission of accompaniment, staying with the refugees who had recently returned to their land. "I'll think of you, much as you thought of me on your trip," I wrote.

I was strickened by the loss of her and dislocated in myself. Still in a daze I managed to resume my responsibilities. The round of work, home chores, and summer visitors provided stability and structure.

I needed therapy but I wasn't ready for a relationship with Shirley. I didn't look at her; I was angry that she wasn't Sally. I wondered how she could think she could take Sally's place. Shirley and I met once a week for fifty minutes. The chaos continued. I stammered about my dual relationship with Sally, how we collaborated in professional and political work, how we looked forward to being friends when therapy ended.

I said that I pushed against Sally's boundaries, that I made a mess between us and hurt our relationship. The mess was mine because I enjoyed being with her. "I need you but I'm afraid to make the same mess," I said.

"Long term work is often a mess. If we work together for a long time there will likely be messes, but we'll be able to work them out. The process will not be perfect," Shirley explained.

Shirley heard me. I sensed her firm, kind strength. She said that we would have no contact outside of this room.

I felt like an abandoned child and worried that I might never see Sally again. Her loving words had slipped away and I couldn't find them. Rocking back and forth I rubbed my face, trying to ease my grief.

Knowing that Sally needed her energy for herself helped me to cope with her absence. Nonetheless, I couldn't manage the irrational thoughts that condemned me as a bad person who should be punished.

The director of the School of Social Work asked me if I would teach the advanced practice course in mental health because Sally was ill. I agreed. Teaching the course would be one more way to keep my connection with Sally, and friendships at the school were rich and supportive.

"It's something you can do," Shirley said when I talked about teaching. I noticed that I was beginning to hear and remember more of Shirley's words.

With only two sessions left before my trip to Guatemala I decided to tell Shirley what we disclosed to Sally. Amidst bizarre laughing and face rubbing I told the story of my life as I now understood it, including childhood trauma and multiple alters.

Someone scratched my arm furiously. "It's important to keep this space safe," Shirley said. The scratching stopped.

"You're brave to have shared so much. Do you wonder if I want to work with you?" she asked.

"Yes," I whispered.

"I do. I've learned to work with people who have your kind of distress," she responded. I was still not able to look at her but I was touched by her listening and empathy.

I dreamt of Sally. In one dream she held my hand and comforted me while speaking of her cancer. I dreamt of her death and the mourning of her children. In one powerful dream we were in the office for our last session and I saw an etching on the wall that I hadn't noticed before. The picture showed black caves on a white background. Two figures stood in front of the largest cave. I told Sally that the figures reminded me of our journey. She stood behind me and hugged me gently. I pressed her hand to my cheek. I was trying to say goodbye. "The dream came from a place deep within you," Shirley observed.

"I miss Sally. "

"Of course you do," she said.

"I listen to your words. They matter to me," I told her. I apologized for my laughing and face rubbing and my inability to look at her.

"Your behavior is okay. You'll look at me when you're ready," she answered.

My journey to Guatemala was a powerful experience. Our delegation traveled first to the remote highland village of Victoria. I felt raw and vulnerable. The beauty of the country consoled me; the hovering mountains, lush flowers and abundant cornfields inspired hope. I witnessed the extraordinary courage of the Mayan people as they rebuilt their community. With them, I washed my clothes in the river.

At night the frightening sounds of gun fire told me that the war was far from over.

A few of us climbed the arduous mountain trail to the tiny settlement of Cuarto Pueblo. Carlos showed us where brutal massacres took place. I saw the gutted out church, the remains of a school, and broken bones in a newly discovered mass grave.

Katrina told us that she fled the attacking army and gave birth to her third daughter in the mountains. She managed to escape with her children to the refugee camp in Mexico. Maria brushed away tears as she spoke of the deaths of her husband and child. The suffering of these brave people was almost unimaginable.

I had so much to learn from them. I wanted to know how to survive the war against my body and how to endure the loss of a cherished friend.

I thought of Sally every day and sent her a postcard with a picture of Rigoberta Menchu. Like her, Sally has spent her life working for peace and human rights.

I returned home. Not hearing from Sally became a sharp pain in me. I could no longer listen to friends speak of their visits with her. Her silence felt like a condemnation.

"I won't be able to resolve my issues with Sally," I said to Shirley.

"You can work them out with me," Shirley responded. "Are you ready to say goodbye to her?"

"I have to be. Sally fulfilled her contract with me. I can't ask for more." But I couldn't deny to myself that I wanted more. I wanted to see her.

Sitting in the room with Shirley was excruciating. At any moment I could be flooded by memories of Sally and become awash with tears. I wanted to get rid of it all: my memories of her, my journal, drawings, and dolls. I fantasized about throwing everything in a box and hurling it into the ocean.

I wondered if I knew Sally at all. When I recalled her many absences, anger surged in me. "It's good that you allow yourself a full range of feelings towards Sally, and that you don't cover things up, recalling only the good moments," Shirley commented. But I felt disloyal when I was angry, I thought to myself.

I was obsessed with the ragged edges of my therapy with Sally. To endure the pain I shut down, mechanically going through each day and forgetting my dreams. Not for a moment could I shake the fear of falling apart. There was no exit from my loss, anger, and regret. Myrna deeply felt the loss of Sally and joined me in grieving.

AUTUMN 1994

Shirley sits next to me on the couch
in the therapy room. "It's okay to lean
on me," she says. I relax against her.

(Dream: November 13,1994)

Driving to my appointment with Shirley on a gray September morning I inserted the tape that Sally made for me before she left for her trip to Mexico and Guatemala. I wept at the sound of her voice and came to a stop on the dirt shoulder of the road. During the past weeks I was only conscious of my awful anger that distanced us; now I remembered her care.

As I climbed the steps to Shirley's office, I promised myself that I would look at her and see how she looked at me. She untied and took off her running shoes, and sat with her legs crossed under her. Her hair was walnut brown. Round wire rimmed glasses framed her eyes. My eyes closed.

"I'm trying to help myself. I'm trying to remember what Sally taught me," I stammered.

Voices clamored with words of sorrow and helplessness. Shirley's voice came from a great distance. "All your feelings are welcome here," she said kindly.

"I dreamt of being trapped in a small town by a mountain of ice," I confided.

"It can melt," she replied.

One bright September afternoon I received a note from Sally. "One day at a time has taken on new meaning for me," she wrote. Now that the radiation was completed she was feeling better, but she was absorbed in all the preoccupations of living with cancer. She thanked me for the quilt and called me friend.

"Do you think she'll let me visit?" I asked Shirley.

"This is new territory. You can't erase the fact that until recently you were Sally's client. "But," she considered, "you also had another relationship. Perhaps she's as confused as you are."

With trepidation and hope I sent Sally a card asking if I might visit with her. The waiting began.

My therapy with Shirley suffered the irresolution of the past. I feared that everything might be perceived as manipulative or borderline behavior, even the admission that our sessions were a comfort.

"How did you interpret Sally's opinion that some of your attitudes and behaviors were borderline?" she asked.

"As something bad," I responded.

"As things to change," Shirley offered.

I clung to the corner of the couch. Shirley asked about members of the system. A voice exploded, "Don't talk about us." Opening the system to Shirley felt daunting, but Jeannie decided to take the risk.

"I want to draw a picture for Sally and write a letter," she said excitedly.

"Naturally you do, but that would be about therapy and therapy with Sally is ended," Shirley said kindly but firmly. Jeannie wiped her eyes and receded.

"You've taken a big step today," Shirley encouraged me.

"At least I'm not at the beginning," I responded.

"You're beginning with me," she replied.

I was ashamed of my fragmentation. Shirley said that we had worked together for only a brief time and that my feelings were understandable. Her empathy was soothing. I struggled to experience her as she was, without wanting her to be Sally.

Shirley explained that she didn't have physical contact with her clients. I wondered if she was protecting herself from me.

Whereas I once drew comfort from Sally's holding me, I now drew comfort from Shirley's voice. Her words fell into me like water on parched land.

The stunning illuminations and mysterious hues of the October light were a blessing. My class was full of curious and inspiring students. It progressed smoothly. Speaker taught, helping the students explore clinical methods and case examples. The huge discrepancy between her competence and my fragility was entirely hidden.

Summoning my courage, I finally brought Baby to therapy and told Shirley about the solace Baby provided me. The moment was broken by alters without names who roared about knives and hurting people.

"It must be hard to have such thoughts," Shirley observed.

I absorbed her compassion, both needing and fearing this new therapeutic relationship. "I'm trying to do therapy without a relationship to you. Many of us are afraid you'll leave. Maybe Sally left because of what we said," I said anxiously.

"It's sad that Sally became sick and had to go away," Shirley replied. "I'm not leaving. Other people have told me painful things and I haven't left."

I wanted to believe her.

Sally's answer arrived in mid-October. She wouldn't meet with me. Her hands were full and she wanted to keep her life simple. "I respect the work you're doing with Shirley and I don't want to muddle it," she wrote, "but it's always good to get news of you from a slight distance."

I showed the note to Shirley. My anger flared in confused, half-formed mutterings. "She doesn't care about us. She lied to us. Why should we open ourselves to you? Did you tell Sally not to meet me. Did both of you laugh about me?"

Shirley listened. "I didn't tell Sally not to meet with you, but I can understand if you don't believe me."

"I want to hurt myself but I don't want to hurt those I love," I said despairingly.

"You would rather die than go through this pain," Shirley observed. "Do you want me to speak with Sally about you?" she asked.

"No." I quickly signed a paper rescinding my earlier permission.

My relationship with Sally became an obsession. Caught between her loving words in the past and her present distance, I sank into self-loathing and hatred toward her. My body sizzled with pain.

With Shirley's encouragement I wrote another letter to Sally requesting a professional meeting so that I could say goodbye. My need for closure was so great that I risked another refusal.

Shirley saw the anguish in me. "When people have a big loss they deal with it in familiar ways. Are you feeling more internal separateness now?"

"Yes," I acknowledged.

"You'll come together when you're ready."

On the last weekend of October, I drove to Boston for a peace conference on solidarity work with Guatemala. I had looked forward to the event and brought with me samples of Woven Lives goods and information about our project. Settling into the crowd in the suburban church, I renewed friendships with old political allies and listened to updates about struggle and hope in Guatemala.

I saw Sally.

She sat a few rows behind me. Her hair was short; she was thin. Stunned, I slowly managed to move my legs and walk toward my car. The din of voices and dishes poured from the open windows of the lunchroom, but I needed to be alone.

Before the afternoon session began the hall buzzed with chatter. From the corner of my eye I saw Sally return to her seat. I approached her, put my arm around her, and bent to kiss her cheek. Her back was hard and bony under her plaid cotton shirt.

"I want to say hello," I murmured. She stared straight ahead.

"I saw you sitting there," she said remotely. There was no acknowledgement of who we had been to each other.

I returned to my seat deeply shaken by the encounter. The conference was a blur. Reaching for my knitting, I felt grateful for the warm gray wool that moved through my fingers.

In the evening I called Myrna. "Saying hello to Sally seemed like the right thing to do, but was it intrusive?" I asked anxiously.

"No. It was human," she said gently.

Desperate for support, I called Shirley and left a message on her machine.

In spite of my anxiety I returned to the conference the next day. Sally sat across the hall. I took in her every gesture and memorized each feature of her presence.

In mid-morning I walked along a deserted hall and saw Sally approaching from the other direction. This was the woman to whom I had poured out my soul. We smiled at each other, saying "hi" as we passed.

From the outside we could have been seen as two political colleagues; from the inside we were two women who shared a deeply intimate process that was not acknowledged.

As the conference ended, she exchanged hugs and goodbyes with many friends. I felt even emptier.

Seeing Sally threw the system into chaos. I dreamt of Daddy throwing a baby against a wall; of being owned by a man in black; of being utterly subjugated to Daddy. Night and day, shame caused havoc. In my next session with Shirley the alters rocked and laughed and shouted about being dirty. Big Barbie dissolved into bizarre laughing.

The clamor of a hundred voices filled my head. I teetered on a precarious edge. My body broke into pieces that spun off into space. Whatever gains I had made toward integration burst apart.

Shirley told me that Sally called her after she received my letter. Shirley told Sally that a final meeting with me would not be untherapeutic. I gave Shirley permission to speak with Sally about this and felt apologetic about my earlier distrust. We agreed that the meeting would be dignified and respectful and that only adult alters would attend.

No goodbye had ever been this crucial.

WINTER 1994 - 1995

Sally and I walk together. I slip my arm
through hers and she does not pull away.

(Dream: December 12, 1995)

In my grief over the loss of Sally I was more connected to the child I was. The utter absence of comfort in my early years felt immediate and wrenching.

My psychic world was changing. I began to fear trees and believed that they would uproot themselves and attack me. I tried to convince myself that this was physically impossible. Still, I didn't look at the trees. The fear stayed with me.

One morning I stepped out of the shower and I felt like a giant in a miniaturized world. Shirley explained that the world could seem different to people who dissociate. I was okay, I told myself.

The fear of losing my mind was ever-present. "Could a psychotic part of me have created the alters and their memories?" I asked Shirley.

"Do you think an unstable part could have had the control to create a two-fold system including parts like Big Barbie and Speaker? Can you imagine that Listener with all her skills, is a product of a disoriented alter?" I was grateful for her reassurance.

"A bomb has fallen on me. The buffer between me and the trauma feels gone. Sally said that we had finished working on the abuse, but more feelings are surfacing," I mumbled.

"We are working on a deeper level. How does this situation connect to the past?" she asked.

"I was open and vulnerable with Daddy. He hurt me and left. I was a client to Sally, not a person. She hurt me and left. " I reached for Baby and covered her with the soft blanket that Shirley handed me.

"Do you feel abandoned?" she asked.

"I don't feel connected to you or to Sally. Connection equals pain," I replied.

Shirley sighed. I had come to accept her sighs as expressions of understanding. "We can work together even if you feel this way,"she said.

I waited for Sally's letter and felt more despairing as the days rolled into weeks. Each day I scanned the mail for her response. Waiting wore me down. "She hates me," I told Shirley.

"What makes you think that Sally hates you?" she asked.

"Because I'm bad. She knows bad things about me."

"You're afraid that I'll think bad things about you if you talk with me," Shirley said.

"Yes," I responded.

"That feeling of being bad goes very deep," she observed. I turned to look out the window.

Light snow fell as I drove home. Maybe I should end therapy; or maybe I should find someone else to work with me, someone who didn't know Sally. It pained me that Shirley could speak to Sally, but I wasn't allowed that same privilege. I blurted out my misgivings to Shirley.

"We'll never have the special intense kind of relationship that you and Sally created," she said. "It was the first time you opened yourself as a multiple and you were the first person with MPD that Sally worked with," she said calmly.

I was too devastated by loss to speak.

"We'll create something different between us. You're not the first person with MPD that I've worked with. I'm pleased by the work we're doing and want to continue. It's the specialness you had with Sally and the complications in the relationship that cause problems for you now."

Her words communicated kindness, compassion, and commitment. Still, I couldn't speak.

By mid-December everyday life tilted on the rim of a volcano. Tony, a trusted friend, suggested I go to an inpatient setting to work through my loss of Sally. Shirley made the alternate suggestion that I find a place near her office for a couple of weeks and have frequent sessions. "There's no obvious right choice. In a hospital there'd be more staff but they'd be unfamiliar with you, and you have a problem with trust. But, the hospital would give you a place to collapse. You need to get out of crisis in order to be stable for the long process," she said.

Myrna and I considered the options.

I decided to apply for a ten-day stay in a private psychiatric hospital. Shirley supported my decision and composed a thoughtful and respectful summary of our work. Not wanting anyone at work to know the truth, I marked the ten days as vacation.

But I continued to struggle with ambivalence. Shirley assured both me and the young, fearful alters that the therapists at the hospital would be safe and helpful. "Perhaps this experience will be a turning point," she added.

When I set out for the hospital, Maine was in the grip of a blizzard. The snow was heavy and relentless. Visibility was poor. My knuckles on the wheel were white with strain. A windshield wiper gave out after a few hours. I pulled off the road and fixed it with a paper clip. Seven hours later I drove into a motel, exhausted by the drive and my mounting fears.

The next day was bright. Sun glittered on the snow. Plows had done their work and only black puddles remained on the road. Six hours later I saw the large brick buildings and sloping snow-covered hills.

Soft upholstered chairs, plush carpets, and restful colors put me at ease in the admission area. The psychiatrist, a large, imposing man, summoned me to a small office. I sat with my eyes closed talking about Sally.

"Your eyes are closed," he commented.

"Yes. I feel safer this way," I replied.

"What else do you get with your eyes closed?" he queried.

"You aren't there," I replied. "I don't like being in a small room with a man."

"What's your fantasy?" he asked.

"That you will hurt me and hit me," I answered.

"It's good that you can say that," he said.

I felt exposed. He asked many questions about my history, my behaviors, and my feelings. "Why do you want to be here?" he asked.

"I need to gain stability and to work through the loss of Sally. I'd like to participate in groups. I can't do that in the rural area where I live." My hand reached in my pocket for my rosary beads. Two weeks ago I dug them out of an old box, hungry for the balm they provided.

"I think you're the kind of person who can work this out. A hospital stay would benefit you," he added. I left the office while he called the insurance company.

In fifteen minutes he summoned me again. The insurance carrier refused to pay for my treatment. "You have to be homicidal or suicidal to be admitted," the psychiatrist said. "You deserve treatment, but I can't say that you're a danger to yourself or others."

The walls of the tiny room slammed against me. I felt humiliated and angry -neither sick enough nor well enough.

At a roadside phone, with eighteen wheelers roaring by, I called Shirley. We agreed to meet for ninety-minute sessions twice this week and three times next week.

After thirteen exhausting hours on the road, I was back in Maine. I registered at a moderately priced motel a few minutes from Shirley's office. Perhaps this arrangement would be better for me.

I slept fitfully, and I dreamt about terror and devastation. Four hours remained until my session.

"Sally kept me safe. The world is different now," I told Shirley.

"When a little girl is learning to skate she holds someone's hand and falls less often; when she's ready she lets go and skates alone. It's the child that does the skating and you who kept yourself safe," Shirley said.

"I don't know where Sally begins and ends. When she got sick, parts of me felt that they would die. Being separate from Sally is being separate from myself. With Sally gone, I don't exist," I stammered.

"It wasn't safe when you were a child. You couldn't take steps in development. Then, you had a powerful attachment to Sally. Now, we can have a connection," she asserted.

"I want you to understand what it's like for me," I insisted.

"No one can completely understand another person. There's an element of mystery in each one of us. Parts of your system have magical thinking. When we resolve that, you'll see that Sally and you are separate; that you can be separate and connected," she explained.

Shirley was in the convent for six years, I recalled. Perhaps I could trust her. Perhaps she would not hate me. Perhaps she could help.

During these intense sessions I struggled to work through my feelings for Sally. "We shared a commitment to a process," I told Shirley. "She was a good enough therapist and I was a good enough client. Why am I suspicious of her words of love for me?"

"You're in a vulnerable position. You seem to assume that there's something wrong with you," Shirley replied.

"I imagine consuming Sally, taking her into myself and making her mine. Maybe I can accept that when she said she loved me, she really meant it." This perspective brought some relief from the suffocation of doubt.

"The real question is about the work we did, not if she loved me," I continued. "Sally did keep her commitment to our process." More relief came with this insight.

At the motel I spread my paper, pens, and crayons over the empty bed. Young alters wrote notes of farewell to Sally. Some drew pictures of her sailing away on her boat. Others slashed the paper with vivid red and black lines. I wrapped myself in my down jacket against the winter cold and took long walks.

There was no word from Sally.

At my next meeting with Shirley my hands rushed to my face in a frenzy of rubbing. "You can't get your face clean because nothing is there. You're trying to erase your history, to rub it off. The rubbing is a sign that you're still in the past," Shirley said. "We need to bring you into the present."

Voices rose in me and quivered. I was reluctant to keep talking about trauma. Sally said that it could be addictive. Shirley listened to my confusions.

"Everyone who has suffered trauma has trauma addiction. Talking about trauma releases certain chemicals in the brain that have a soothing effect. People can get addicted to that experience," she explained. "But what's happening here has nothing to do with addiction," she added.

On January 26, I received a note from Sally. She had intended to meet with me after Christmas but she suddenly became very ill. It was final: I would never see her again.

In early February I wrote a last note to her, lingering over each word. I included a pair of my hand-knit wool socks which she liked so much.

Alters regressed into painful memories. Mary shouted about perpetrators watching her in the room. "You can see through them," Shirley advised. "Tell them to go to work, play cards or listen to the radio."

"I hate them to talk about the cult," I admitted.

"Is there any reason why it would be good to talk about it?" Shirley wondered.

"Yes. The cult still has power over my mind and body."

"You have many pieces. We need to bring them together. Some alters have pieces that make sense of other pieces. Our main work is to bring the pieces together and tell the story of your history," Shirley explained. "When it becomes a story, it becomes a memory. Some alters are relieved when they tell their stories and the alters who listen feel relief to hear the stories. Alters can also learn about good memories. Most of you is still in the past."

On Valentine's Day, Sally's birthday, I sent her an arrangement of daisies, a flower that had always delighted her.

Alters regressed further. I had headaches every day.

"Sometimes when people are faced with a crisis in the present they return to trauma in the past," Shirley said. "You went deep in therapy with her. It isn't finished. You are a grieving woman. Rest, have fewer expectations of yourself."

Therapy became a shelter in a terrible emotional storm. But I couldn't look at Shirley and I didn't remember her face. In my dreams a therapist was a ghostly figure.

"Maybe your dreams are about being in-between. You're not finished working through your feelings about Sally and you're beginning work with me. What do you need to do?"

I collapsed on the couch, clutching Baby. "Baby is strong and flexible," Shirley said.

"But the Blackness. The Blackness is overtaking me. My legs and body burn," I sputtered.

"You are wearing blue today. Remember the blue," Shirley said, urging me to remain grounded in the present.

My fears leapt like flames around me. Shirley said that I was too close to the edge. The prospect of falling apart loomed like a frightening extinction.

SPRING 1995

It's Easter. I'm in Sally's house with a group of people. The rooms are bathed in light. A small tree covered with pastel blossoms grows from the center of a room.

(Dream: March 17, 1995)

In early March, Shirley brought me a green crate containing the papers, dreams, drawings, and notes I gave to Sally. "She gave me a message for you. Let me know when you're ready to hear it," Shirley said.

I nodded.

"She said that she loves you; that in all the dimensions of your relationship she learned from you. She's at peace in her relationship with you. Sally looks beautiful. She's on a spiritual journey," Shirley said slowly.

My hands covered my face. "Draw on whatever spiritual sense you have to help yourself," Shirley encouraged.

In my study I took out the folders one by one from the green crate. Amidst dreams and drawings I discovered cards I had sent her. I found only a few notations on our work. She was lost to me.

I braided kernels of black corn and an amethyst onto black Guatemalan thread to create a bracelet of mourning.

In therapy I felt that the windows, doors, and pictures would attack me. At home I sensed lurking presences ready to pounce on me.

These feelings flowed from Chair who couldn't discriminate between animate and inanimate reality. Shirley explained that Chair and possibly other alters experienced primary process thinking. "In this way of thinking, contradictions coexist; there isn't any conception of time or logical connections between ideas. If Chair thinks something, she believes that it's real." Shirley taught Chair to say, "Windows be still; doors be still." She encouraged me to have compassion for the parts of myself that suffered a distorted reality. "All of you are having feelings that you've never had before."

"There's more internal communication as the alters share feelings of grief. We are enduring this loss together," I said. How strange, I thought to myself, that Sally's death could be a thread that wove us together.

On March 19th, I attended a meeting to organize against a referendum that would prohibit civil rights for lesbians and gay men in Maine. A colleague turned to me. "Did you hear that Sally died last night?"

Returning home, I told Myrna and fell into bed. I sobbed until I was exhausted and finally fell asleep.

In the morning I learned that our friend Sandy had called to tell us about Sally's death. Myrna had written it all down for me. "She died at nine o'clock Saturday night with her children around her bed. Her death was peaceful. The children stayed with her throughout the night."

I stopped eating.

On Monday I was incapable of working. I carefully framed a picture of a Goddess holding a child in her arms. I made the matt from pieces of the Guatemalan cloth that Sally gave me and I put dried daisies from Sally's bouquet to Jeannie along one edge. The picture was beautiful and soothing. I hung it in my study.

I drove to Sally's house, something I had never done before, because I needed to see where she had lived and died. It was just as she described it: a small coastal house with weathered shingles, the pond where the otter played, bay windows that let in the light, and the flower and vegetable gardens beyond the rear deck.

The garage door was open. I was startled by the brown wheelchair leaning against the door. Her illness was real. Her death was real.

I found in the local newspaper a long obituary describing her many accomplishments and sent copies to a few friends out of state.

No map existed for a client whose therapist had died. Our therapeutic relationship defined the intimacy between us, but it existed in a private world. I couldn't grieve with her close friends and relatives. As her client, I was part of Sally's life only in a minimal professional way. Except for Myrna, Shirley, and a few friends, I grieved in isolation.

Retreating into myself seemed like the only way to get through each day. Myrna observed that I wasn't talking. Sally was dead and so was I.

On the seventh day I began to eat.

At the memorial my eyes fixed on the blue urn containing her ashes. The church was overflowing. I couldn't look at anyone, nor could I speak. Mourners sang and prayed; family and friends told stories about her life. Friends squeezed my hand or patted my shoulder.

Shirley gave me a poem - "the ashes hold the form." "Don't give up on yourself," she said. "There's an important learning trying to take root in you. You'll get to something solid in yourself."

"My head feels enlarged; my hands seem huge," I told her. "I'm lost. My body aches from the cracks and splinters. There's nothing but chaos."

"Open your eyes. I'm available to you," she urged.

"You can look through me if I look at your eyes. I'm afraid I'll see that you hate me," I mumbled.

"I can't see inside of you. You can look at me and protect yourself. Looking at me can help you stay grounded. Two things are going on: the death of Sally and your experience of nonbeing. Think of the experience of nothingness as what is going on between you and me," she said.

My thoughts were confused and chaotic. My feelings for Shirley raced from a terrible fear, to dependence and affection.

Life felt like a series of disconnected moments. The dread of something yet unseen unnerved me. I watched Listener carefully interact with her therapy clients and was grateful for her skill. Shirley pointed out that Listener was me.

In a startling dream I heard a voice call," Come deeper; come deeper."

Losing Sally was an earthquake. More damaged parts of me presented themselves to Shirley. "Parts of you only know a reality in which everything is scarey. They think that things will assault them. Perhaps we could pair strong parts with fragile alters. " This plan seemed promising and we adopted it. Chair, Alice, and Rain joined with Jane, Ella, and Big Barbie.

I told Shirley that when she acknowledged our feelings, even the frightening ones, and didn't try to change them, but accepted how bad we felt, that she helped us.

"Our relationship is a kind of container that you can use. We're trying to braid together your relationship with Sally, your fear of a relationship with me, and the trauma of the alters," she said.

Sessions tumbled over with scared voices. Some alters laughed; others shouted about knives. I sank into depression. Jeannie and Hope were afraid that Barbara would end therapy. "Barbara can do therapy this time so it won't boomerang on her," Shirley replied.

"I'm afraid of attaching to Shirley," I told Anne, a close friend. She looked thoughtfully at me. "Your therapy is your spiritual practice. Let go of your fear. Accept that Sally loved you and that she was unable to say goodbye. " My heart struggled to open.

My personal memorial to Sally was a small lilac bush that I planted at the edge of our perennial garden. When we left her office after our last session, she had pointed out a beautiful lilac bush and we had both breathed in the sweet fragrance.

In preparation for a pilgrimage to Crete that Myrna and I planned to make, I turned to writings about the Great Mother. She encompassed benevolence and cruelty, good and evil. I thought of Sally's strengths and her fallibility. "Not saying goodbye to me was a therapeutic error," I said to Shirley.

"That must be hard for you to admit," she responded.

"Why do I talk about Sally so much," I asked her.

"Don't you think you have a lot to work through?"

"Yes. Thanks for hanging in. Working with me is like Mission Impossible," I joked.

"They always accepted the mission and it turned out okay," she quipped back. "It's not hard to hang in with you."

"We never shared some of the frightening feelings with Sally," I murmured.

"Sally was new to this work; it was a precious learning together that you had."

I fingered the mourning bracelet on my wrist.

SUMMER 1995

> I see a little girl encased in wood. Only her head and neck are visible. Someone is cutting the wood away. I worry that she'll be hurt.
>
> (Dream: August 1, 1995)

With ten other women, Myrna and I set out for a pilgrimage in Crete led by Carol Christ. Carol is a thealogian whose work is dedicated to bringing the Goddess tradition to women. My anticipation deepened as I studied Minoan culture and discovered multiple images of the Goddess.

The beauty of the island -- a stunning collage of olive trees, grape vines, bouganvillea, and white stone houses -- fed my soul. In this exquisite pastoral setting, goats roamed the mountains and sheep were herded across narrow streets. Sky and water radiated blue beauty.

Carol incorporated rituals into our journey. We created altars with symbolic personal objects. I offered broken shells from our beach; Myrna contributed spruce cones and bird feathers. Other women arranged jewelry, Goddess images, and fruits on the altar stone. We poured simple libations of milk, water or honey, joined our voices in chant, and told our stories.

Out of concern for the alters, I continued to pair vulnerable parts of the system with strong, present-oriented members. Protector took special responsibility for the overall arrangement. We held together.

The pilgrimage was full of amazing surprises. In centuries-old monasteries, convents and chapels, I felt drawn to icons of Mary. She was the Blessed Mother of my childhood. Now as my eyes met hers on ancient canvas, She became the Mothersoul in whom I live, the Great Mother who had never left me.

In the small gift store attached to the Panagia convent, dedicated to the preservation of an old, sacred myrtle tree, I found a beautiful image of Mary. Her eyes were sorrowful but fearless. To my great joy I also found a picture of St. Barbara. I had not seen her image for over forty years. I clutched these treasures and rejoined the group for thick Greek coffee and cookies in the large convent parlor.

Our travels took us to Feistos and Knossus where we explored neolithic ruins. I was inspired by the pithoi, large clay pots which were used for food storage. Some of these pots were pieced together with cement and strong wire. I stood next to a pot, bigger than myself, and Myrna snapped a picture. Later that evening she slipped a poem into my hand.

TRAVELING WITH A SURVIVOR

In the museums, you are drawn
to pieced-together pithoi, those tall
clay vessels Minoans used for storage.

You want to trace with your fingers
the fissure marks. The huge staples
inside the vessel feel like the
stitches you use to pull the fragments
of your life together, to hold yourself
steady in any given reeling day.

Out of desperation, out of love,
I want to fashion you
with my bare hands, find the clay
and haul the water, turn the wheel
with my feet, lift you up
from the pull of gravity
into a vessel that can hold
your soul, gather rain water,
store provisions you will need
on your way. I would fashion a lip
for pouring wine and honey and water
over rock altars, a handle graceful
as a gazelle, body curved, womanly,
capable, enduring.
Instead, I take a picture of you
standing beside a pithos almost
as tall as you, decorated with clay
ropes and starshapes, all the seams
of patching visible, standing
by virtue of steel sutures hidden
inside. But standing, capable,
enduring.

Tears wet my cheeks. We slipped into bed and held each other tenderly in the warm night.

One sunny afternoon we descended slowly into the Skoteino cave guided by Mr. Nikos, a cheerful, sturdy man in his sixties whose knowledge of the cave was legendary. Archeologists hypothesized that this and other neolithic caves were places where people lived, worshipped, and buried their dead.

We walked single file, holding lighted tapers. The path was narrow, slippery, and dangerously steep. At hazardous points, Mr. Nikos showed each one of us where to place our feet. At the second level a few women chose to stop. It was risky to go further. I felt afraid, but Myrna whispered, "You can do it."

We descended into darkness black as tar, weaving our way past sharp rocks and haunting stalagmites. Large stalactites dripped from overhead.

At the fourth level, the bottom of the cave, we extinguished our candles. The darkness was unlike anything I'd ever known. We sat on the floor and I leaned against an immense stalagmite. I felt Her in this solid form, holding me in this pitch-black world. A belief formed in my soul: there is no place I can enter, even in the furthest reaches of my mind, where She will not be.

Toward the end of the journey, we traveled to the Lasithi Plains, an area known for strenuous resistance against the German invasion in the Second World War. At the local tavern the owner read poems about peace written by his brother. I felt blessed to be in this place that had a history of such courage.

Leaving the tavern we hiked up the long, dusty road to the Idean Cave. Suddenly I felt things growing from my arms and hands. My face felt bloody and bruised. For a moment I rubbed myself frantically. Then I reminded myself that these were feelings, not reality. When I looked at my hands and touched my face, I could see that they were clean.

According to legend, Gaia hid her son Zeus in this cave because she feared that his father would kill him. The mouth of the cave was wide; wooden stairs made it possible to descend to the lower level. Large, dark rooms spread out from the cave's center.

When I ran my hand over the coal-black walls, words from scripture came to mind, "Blessed is the womb that bore you." At this sacred moment I experienced myself as a daughter of the earth. Never had I felt such communion with the natural world.

With a grateful heart I walked with sister-pilgrims into a side chamber of the cave. A woman began to chant "Light and Darkness" and our voices joined with hers. I stopped. My right hand moved over my heart and my left hand rested on my belly. Light and darkness. My breasts felt like mountains filled with light. My lower body was a cave of mystery.

Light and shadows. Good and evil. Both were real. I held them in myself.

When we returned to Maine we placed our precious Goddess figures on our altar. One radiated peace; a second raised her arms in joy; a third image evoked death and resurrection.

Returning to therapy, I wanted to draw even more meaning from the journey. "If She is my Mother and I am Her daughter how can I not be good?" I asked Shirley.

"You are good," she said positively.

"There was a startling moment in the Elitheian cave, a place associated with the Goddess of childbirth. I became aware that the roots of my life are deeper than my own life. My roots are in Her," I told Shirley. "She contains my whole story."

"The pilgrimage was healing for you," she responded.

"Yes, it was a sacrament," I replied.

While I was on my absorbing pilgrimage my first grandchild was born. David and Tina named him Martin. When the family gathered for his christening in late June I fell in love with this beautiful baby. He wore the white lace baptismal dress that I had made for all my children. David's face radiated with love as he held his infant son. I offered a prayer of thanksgiving.

In therapy I lay exhausted on the couch. "The alters and their feelings are bursting out. There's no containment. That takes energy from you," Shirley said. "The alters can go to their inside rooms where they'll be safe. Each of them will have a turn to come here and talk." Her words calmed the pressing impulses of impatient parts of myself.

I confided to Shirley that I had a hard time letting her matter to me in the same way that Sally mattered. "You can use me," she replied.

"It helps us when I lie on the couch and we listen to your voice. Having your voice inside makes us feel better," I said.

An unexpected moment of healing occurred when Myrna and I met Shirley and her friends at the Bangor Gay Pride parade. We waved at each other. Shirley and her partner Ginny spoke easily with us. Shirley introduced us to her mother, a white haired woman with a lovely soft face. Those few minutes were relaxed, friendly, and respectful. They seemed to ease an ache in my relationship with Sally caused by her coolness at our final chance encounter.

"I don't know what was real with Sally. I wish she had said goodbye to me," I told Shirley.

"The therapy relationship was real. I wish she had said goodbye to you, too," Shirley replied. "I have a few thoughts about this and I'll share them with you when you want to hear them. I don't want to interrupt your flow of feelings," she added.

"Please let me hear them."

"You and Sally had a dual relationship. You were friends, and at the same time she was your therapist and you were her client. Sally seemed to come to a point where she recognized that her relationship with you was essentially that of therapist and client. When she became seriously ill she felt that she couldn't meet with you as your therapist," Shirley explained. "These are my perceptions, not things that Sally told me," she added.

"Thank you. I'll think about what you said."

During these warm July days I struggled with doubts about the alters' reports of ritual abuse. I didn't want to believe that my father could have done this to me. The professional debate about recovered memory added fuel to my resistance. I needed to find a way to proceed in therapy despite my misgivings. A compromise occurred to me: I could accept the alters' reports as emotional and psychic truth, not necessarily as literal truth.

"Why don't you ask the alters how they feel about it," Shirley suggested.

We gathered in the internal conversation room. The alters protested my compromise. They asked if I would accept their disclosures about ritual abuse for the next six months, and then meet for another discussion. I cautiously agreed.

When I told Shirley about this plan, Mimi popped out asking whether Shirley would go away.

"I've heard stories before about ritual abuse and I haven't gone away. I won't go away now," she said.

Traumatized alters emerged - some who feared the cult and others who felt satisfaction in following the rules. In one session, my body shook with intense agitation until Cecilia took over. "I calm the body just as I did in the cult when I submitted to their orders," she said slowly.

When she receded a tremor surged through me. "What if it's true?"

Peril appeared. "I'm glad Barbara had that feeling. She has to feel it."

"Were you abused?" Shirley asked.

Peril was stunned by the question. "I protected the others. I've always been tall and strong. " She hesitated, shifting her body on the couch.

Shirley waited.

"We're all one body, aren't we?" Peril queried, sensing the implications. "If it happened to them, then, in some way it also happened to me."

"Yes," Shirley said softly.

"I need to think about this," Peril replied.

"It's important to remember that just as bad things happened, good things happened, too," Shirley said. "The good and bad need to be woven together. " Peril nodded and withdrew.

I seemed to have crossed a critical line into a different psychological world. Walls laughed at me. Books and lamps mocked me. I had more terrifying dreams. I lay silently on the couch in the therapy room.

"You can say everything you want and need to say," Shirley said.

"I need to learn to take care of myself. Sally couldn't take care of me. Myrna can't. You can't," I protested.

I curled into a fetal position. The room was coming after me. Pictures and chairs hurled themselves at me. "I don't know where I am," I mumbled.

"I understand," Shirley replied.

Moaning and laughing sounds tumbled from my mouth.

"You're learning to understand how you helped each other," she explained.

Alters shouted about being bad, about bad spirits. Some yelled that Satan was bad. Others screamed that Satan was good. The emotional turbulence eventually subsided. I could hear Shirley say that it was important to come into the present. "This is hard but you'll find ways to cope," she encouraged me.

During the last meeting before Shirley's vacation, Barbara Davis came forward. "I heard what happened to Peril. There's only one body. If an alter was abused then I was abused, too," she said. "I never thought I was abused. I wanted to have a good daddy. I prayed and asked for God's help. God must have known that Daddy hurt us. Maybe God gave us the grace to survive," she added.

Shirley observed that Barbara Davis's eyes brimmed with tears. "You have something special to give to the system. You can help them grieve," Shirley said gently.

I told Shirley that there were times when I denied my multiplicity, but hearing Barbara Davis increased my understanding of having different parts. "Her feelings and experiences are remarkably clear," I said.

Driving home I thought of God and Barbara Davis. The Great Mother had always known who I was. Now I was learning to know myself as She knew me.

AUTUMN 1995

> I'm lying on the floor cradling a baby.
> Slowly I drop juice into the baby's mouth.
> Shirley watches me.
>
> (Dream: November 17, 1995)

On the way to Boston I stopped at the cemetery in southern Maine where Sally's ashes would be interred. Red and gold maple leaves were a sharp contrast to the dull gray headstones. The cemetery was old. Sally's father and other ancestors were buried here. I sat on the grass and touched the earth where she would be placed. Comforting myself, I remembered that our relationship was more than the hard ending.

Sally visited me in dreams. She told me to talk about her death. She held me or walked silently beside me. I wondered if she was letting me know that there was peace between us.

Child alters didn't understand her absence. They asked Shirley when Sally would return. "Sally became sick and died. She isn't coming back. I'm your therapist now," she explained.

Sandy, a close friend, gave me two boxes of books and notes that Sally had left to her. The material was from Sally's classes on mental health and community organizing. These were the classes that I now taught. I lifted out papers and saw her graceful writing. Holding her notes and books close to me seemed to make her present. Suddenly, my feelings of love changed to hate. She left me. I had never felt such hate before.

Days later I recognized yet again that Sally did not set out to hurt me. She wanted to help me heal. With this belief firmly in place, I finally forgave her and allowed myself to feel the full goodness of our relationship.

I lay on the couch in the therapy room. Shirley said, "You needed to have all of your feelings toward Sally, even the hate. Now there is openness, growth, and change."

The same fears that marked my early relationship with Sally intruded into my relationship with Shirley. Now it was Shirley who would attack and hurt me. But the fears were less powerful. They were about the past. I had learned that trusting another person gave rise to fear of terrible harm.

"Perhaps you could make a decision that no matter what I say, think, or do, that you could still exist. In the past Sally held your safety. Perhaps you can hold it for yourself now," Shirley explained.

My sense of safety in the therapy room grew deeper. For months I had watched Shirley take off her shoes at the beginning of the hour and replace them at the end. "I assume you do that for comfort," I said.

"Yes," she replied.

"It reminds me of how Moses took off his shoes in front of the Burning Bush. This, too, is sacred ground," I said.

A slow smile spread across Shirley's face. "Therapeutic space can be like that," she replied.

I lay on the couch frequently now. "How do you feel about my lying here?" I asked Shirley.

"I remember that you lay on the couch when you rested on Sally's lap," she answered. As I clutched the pillow the sound of Sally's heartbeat came back to me.

By mid-October the couch wasn't enough. I lay on the floor, curling up on a small multi-colored rug. There was nowhere to fall now. I heard Shirley say, "If something can be, it can change." These words encouraged me. When the shadows pursued me, the alters and I thrust our hands against them but our efforts were useless. I felt helpless against the assaultive world. "Everything is scarey to me," I whispered.

"Your insides feel scarey," Shirley said. "You are safe with me."

Darkness, a group of alters, laughed at me. I felt swallowed, annihilated, cracked. I was the earthquake at the core of myself.

"Now that we see the earthquake, maybe we can fix it," Shirley mused, "or maybe we can strengthen the sides so there'll be less crumbling."

At Shirley's suggestion, I told the Darkness that they were also Light. Darkness was not subdued. "We're stronger. We hold the alters that obeyed out of fear of death," I heard them say.

Shirley encouraged me to sit up and look at her. "It's important to contain this work with the Darkness within therapy," she advised. "Strong alters will support you."

We agreed to meet twice a week. I searched for Mud Girl in the closet of my study. Her howling face and dismembered limbs mirrored my brokenness. Oddly, I sensed that she was strong enough to contain the earthquake and prevent dangerous tremors in the wider internal system.

In my quiet hours I turned to my wool to fashion socks for friends. As the yarn took form I considered my therapy. The process, thoughts, and feelings were real. They were connected to something real. It was becoming harder for me to deny the abuse. Perhaps Shirley's acceptance of me made this deeper work possible. Sally and I never went this far inward.

Darkness gripped me. Daddy and his friends surrounded me. "See the images as pictures," Shirley said, "as flat and one-dimensional." She helped me understand the presence of circuits of anxiety in my brain. "With more skill, you'll be able to attach to calm circuits," she explained. Relief was possible, I promised myself.

I was startled when Shirley said, "Your mind is rich. " My mind. My mind belonged to me - not to Daddy or anyone else. I felt stunned by this radical idea and amazed by my own surprise.

By late November the Darkness began to change. Having learned from other alters about the tricks Daddy and his friends played, they moved closer to the present. Some alters feared the Darkness and wanted to keep them separate. "They are already part of us," I told them.

"There's wisdom in the Darkness," Shirley said.

"Yes. I feel that I'm accepting and integrating the evil within myself, a difficult and humbling process." At the same time I recognized more clearly that I could choose how to act; I was not at the mercy of violent internal pressures.

Why, then, did I feel increasingly disorganized? I dreamt of being trapped in my house, threatened by rising waters.

"What stands between you and integration?" Shirley probed.

"Acceptance. I need to affirm that they are me and I am them. They've already revealed their experiences. They're closer to each other and have made many changes. Fear keeps us separate." I resolved to accept my multiple parts. There was no need for division.

Driving home that cold November morning I composed a chant to sing to the alters. "Welcome Jeannie. Welcome Jane. Welcome Teri. Welcome Darkness. . . " The song went on and on.

WINTER 1995-1996

A woman holds a baby over a lamp.
An ornamental spike is on the top
of the shade. She lowers the baby
onto the spike.

(Dream: January 9, 1996)

"I'm in the midst of a controlled breakdown," I told Shirley. "Knives and scissors come at me through the air. I see insects crawling over the floor. I know that they're really not there, but it takes a lot of energy to cope with the images."

"Perhaps as we put your story together these images might make sense in some way. I wonder if you could remind yourself that these feelings and images come from your history?"

For a very long time I had been telling myself that unexpected feelings came from the alters. To say that the source was my history emphasized one body, one history, one self. Pushing my fears aside, I adopted her suggestion. The shift was subtle and remarkable.

Darkness came into therapy again, along with Knight. They worked on experiences of cult violence, subjugation, and forced participation. Shirley showed them a calendar of 1995 as they struggled to grasp present reality.

"I hate this," I told Shirley.

"Of course you do," she replied," but we can't wash over things that were horrible. Some of this may be part of your history and we need to attend to it. "

My mind turned to recent dreams with a recurring theme: I'm being abused in a psychiatric hospital. Then the words tumbled into the room, "Daddy's hospital." Something deep in me came together.

"Daddy's hospital. Daddy's hospital," I repeated over and over. I moved to the floor. I heard words about body holes and things being stuffed in them. One voice whispered, "I was a hole. "

"You were a whole little girl," I heard Shirley say.

I lay on the floor remembering the pages and pages of black holes that the alters and I have drawn over the years.

My driving was threatened by overwhelming feelings. I pulled over to the side of the road in moments of instability.

I told Shirley, "The feeling of disintegration frightens me. It's like being shattered, crushed. There's nothing left; no one behind my voice." She suggested that I take an anti-anxiety medication and I agreed.

I wondered how it was that my mother did not notice that I was sad and withdrawn. My aunt had said that I was never a happy child. My mother said that I was normal.

"Perhaps what she saw was normal for her," Shirley answered. A click went off in my mind.

In mid-December I still required the safety of the floor. As I recounted my recurring dreams of cult activities, my body trembled. Shirley inquired if anyone inside knew about these feelings. I noticed that she always followed her question with: "You may not have an answer. Answer only if you wish."

On one afternoon I seemed to fall into blackness. I rocked back and forth without speaking. I heard Shirley tell me that I was safe. "This is about healing," she said. "This is about making your life work better for you."

Chair emerged. She curled herself into a tight ball. Shirley invited her to open her eyes and look around. Chair was afraid of everything: lamps, pictures, tables. "Look carefully at things," Shirley coaxed.

"They don't move," Chair said as she touched the furniture. Moving around the room she confirmed that things moved only if touched.

"The light goes on only when I turn it on," Shirley said, turning the switch.

Chair noticed a baby doll lying on a pillow. Frantically she piled stuffed animals around the doll to keep it safe. She carefully placed a blanket over the doll.

"Need to keep the baby safe," she said to Shirley.

"What could happen to the baby?" Shirley asked.

"Baby could be hit, have things put in her. Baby could be cut. There's blood on my hands," Chair cried, rubbing her face.

"Look at your hands. There's no blood," Shirley urged. "I'm sorry that this happened to you. When you see things happen it seems like they're happening to you," Shirley said.

"Yes," Chair replied, and disappeared inside to receive special protection.

I lay on the floor. I heard Shirley encourage me to orient myself to the present. I sat up and noticed how Chair had covered the doll. "Why did Chair do this?" I asked.

"Try to rephrase the question: why was it important for me to do this?"

"I know it has to be me because there's one body, but it doesn't feel that way." I looked at the covered doll and wished I could put it in a box to make it even safer.

"What happened is close to the heart of you," Shirley said. "I see you as a whole person who has worked hard to hold together."

I acknowledged to Shirley my attraction to the world of Chair, Rain, Alice, and others. Their world was scarey but if I lived in it I wouldn't have to constantly struggle against it, a kind of surrendering to an altered consciousness.

"Gradually you would lose your freedom, and parts of you wouldn't like that," she warned. "The trauma created physiological changes in your brain. There are well worn grooves connected to terror. The pull toward the world of Chair is seductive," she added.

"It's hard for me to stay in this world," I said.

"I believe you, Barbara," she said empathically.

Although my work at the clinic continued to go well I checked in with Shirley about her perceptions. I wanted to make certain of my competence. "I have confidence in you," she replied. "If I ever had a question about your work I would talk about it with you. I have no questions now."

I felt affirmed and continued to work well.

During the Christmas season I tried to bracket my therapy and enjoy holiday pleasures. The love of family and friends was balm to my soul. I absorbed all the gladness my heart could hold and gave thanks for the deep blessings in my life.

But things changed when I went to Boston to visit my children and grandson. I stayed at the old family house, almost empty now and ready to be sold. On the second night I woke up suddenly feeling that someone was trying to get into bed with me. I felt other people in the room. They were here to get me. My legs burned. Hands held me down. My genitals hurt. If I offended them with my thoughts they would punish me. My face was marked with blood. My body was tied. I lay there unable to move for a long time.

Eventually I turned on the light. I checked my face in the mirror. My face was clean. The house was quiet.

I told Shirley what happened. "They don't want me to talk. I don't want to talk anymore."

"Could this have been a memory or a flashback?" Shirley wondered. "Could the alters have arranged this to make you aware of them?"

"I don't want to integrate alters associated with the cult," I acknowledged. "I want this to go away."

"It isn't working; it isn't going away," she replied.

"I don't want it to be true."

"What would it mean to you if it were true?" Shirley queried.

"That my father was evil. That I am evil, possessed. That I did awful things. I don't want it to be true."

"You're having intense conflict," Shirley observed. "You also feel crazy."

"Yes. I do feel crazy," I responded. "Maybe I've been misdiagnosed."

"Take a normal family, then take a family where incest takes place - that's crazy. If you add cult activity, that's in another realm. What happened was crazy-making," she said.

"I don't have words for it. I can't get my mind around it," I murmured.

I lay on the rug with my hands over my face. I felt like I was dissolving. I remembered words from another therapist, "The disintegration that I fear most has already happened."

I traced my legs, arms, and hands reminding myself that my body was whole and connected.

The question of my history wouldn't go away. "How will I ever know what happened to me?" I asked Shirley at our next session.

"I don't know all that happened to me," Shirley answered. Imagine a little girl in a war. A bomb kills her friend. The little girl has nightmares and dreams that she is bombed. There is more trauma, more fear, and more dreams. The little girl doesn't know how to sort it out. It's not that she's making it up. She has been traumatized."

The story helped me reconcile with the alters who were reporting cult abuse. It was impossible to know everything precisely, but I was more able now to listen closely to them and hear their history.

I lay on the floor covered with a blanket, holding Baby. Shirley wondered if there was anything we needed to do before the alters in the light came together with the alters in the darkness.

"No. We feel ready," I responded. We closed our eyes and went inside. I heard Shirley's voice tell us that we were safe. I saw one circle of figures filled with light and a second circle of figures hidden in shadows. The circles moved toward each other, becoming tangled and chaotic. Gradually, one circle formed, figures of light alternating with dark forms. Protector put blessed water on our palms. We committed ourselves to each other. But there was terror in my body and stuff all over my face. Laughter spurt out. The light was the darkness; the darkness was the light.

I heard Shirley say something about my knowing terror, that it was my history.

"I'm scared, but this is better than pushing parts away. Some of us knew terror; other parts knew how to be calm. We need to live with what we know, not deny it," I said. A sharp pain stung my chest, a wound that was also a healing.

Shirley reminded us to meet internally every day to strengthen the bonds. "Be open to all your feelings," she advised. I drew my feelings with crayons and discovered a dominant theme of chaos.

I tried to sit on the couch, careful to focus my eyes on Shirley. "I want to look at you," I said.

"What makes this important to you now?" she asked.

"I want to take you in. I want to be visible. I need to strengthen the connection between us."

"You close your eyes and go into your internal world. As you look at me you bring your thoughts and feelings into the room with me. You're not alone. When you look at me you increase your openness to the present."

"You have some cognitive distortions," she continued. "For example, 'I am invisible if my eyes are closed.' This is the way a child thinks."

"I also realize that I close my eyes because I fear you might assault me if I look at you. If I close my eyes, I'm not here and you're not here either," I replied.

"I think of it very differently," Shirley said. "If I were afraid of being hurt, I would keep my eyes open to be sure I was safe. But if one is trapped and hurt, it makes sense to go away in whatever way one can."

"I'm here to be your witness," she said. "Therapy is like a platform where you can bring your thoughts, feelings, and experiences."

Our talk returned to darkness and light. She pointed out my deep belief that the dark is stronger than the light.

"Look at your life, Barbara. It's clear that you choose to do good in the world. You could have made other choices."

The integration of light and dark forged new links. Big Barbie, who was not abused, and Cecilia, who participated in the cult, shared their memories. Cecilia found joy in memories of babies, flowers and domestic crafts. Big Barbie was traumatized by the memories of the cult. "I thought I could make Cecilia's memories disappear," she protested. "I don't want them. They didn't happen to me."

"They will fade with time like an old photo," Shirley soothed.

Shirley asked Big Barbie to look at her hands. "In one hand put the memories from Cecilia; in the other, put your own good memories."

Big Barbie hesitated.

"I know it's hard for you to believe that Cecilia's history is also yours," she said. "Look at your hand with memories from Cecilia. Blink three times. Now look at the memories in the other hand. Blink three times." Big Barbie repeated the process a few times. Then, following Shirley's instructions, she folded her hands in her lap.

"Both are together. Both true. You needn't give up either one. Both are your history," Shirley explained.

"I never understood what integration would mean. I always felt strong but now I feel anxious and need help," Big Barbie lamented. Shirley pointed out that Big Barbie was having post-traumatic reactions and that if she couldn't tolerate them she could give the memories back to Cecilia. Big Barbie wasn't sure, but over the next few days she decided to keep the memories. "This is the only way we can all heal," she said. "And besides, we can share good memories, too."

Gradually, Big Barbie became conscious that she was not able to protect the inside children. "I never imagined how horrible it was; I never imagined that the world was so violent."

"What you protected was the hope that love, goodness, and beauty are possible," Shirley said. "You couldn't protect yourself, your body, even parts of your mind."

Big Barbie rocked silently. "How do you mend brokenness?" she asked.

SPRING 1996

I'm a child in a group of strange
people. We're all dressed in black.
My face has black markings. I try
to wash but my right hand disconnects
from my arm.

(Dream: May 29, 1996)

In early March, Myrna and I knew that it was time to put down our cat of eighteeen years. Myrna tied a strand of red yarn, from a Buddhist Refuge Ceremony, around the cat's black and white neck to give her safe passage. She held Cassie as the vet gave the injection and our sweet pet died instantly. I took Myrna in my arms to comfort her in this hard loss. Cassie was her precious cat companion.

March was also the first anniversary of Sally's death. I lit a candle in her memory and wrote her a five-page letter pouring out my sadness, confusion, and affection. She gave me the only maternal love I had ever known.

Jeannie drew pictures of Sally - the good Sally who brought her flowers and the Sally who left her. Turning to Shirley she asked, "Will you promise to say goodbye to me?"

"I can't make that promise," Shirley answered. "The future is uncertain. I do hope that what happened between you and Sally does not happen between us." Jeannie was mildly consoled and returned to her drawings.

I thought about the struggles and healing in my therapy with Sally, and about how different my work was with Shirley.

"This change to you is good for us," I acknowledged. "My dual relationship with Sally caused confusions both inside and outside of therapy. There were things I was afraid to tell her."

"That must be hard for you to say," she answered.

"Yes. I fear I'm being disloyal."

"Think of a child who has a good mother. The child reaches a point where her mother can't give her what she needs. The child goes in search of someone else to help her," Shirley explained.

I liked the story and felt more at peace with my complex feelings.

Memories of my own mother came to the surface. Little Barbie reported that "Sometimes when she was in the bathroom, she'd tie my hands and my sister's hands in paper bags so we wouldn't hit each other. I hated it."

I listened to her and told Shirley about an episode that occurred when I was about eight. "My mother and some of her friends were at the apartment. She gave me money and sent me to the store for cigarettes. On the way home I fell down the wooden stairs next to the railroad tracks. I woke up sprawled in the dirt, dusty and bruised. When I got home I gave the cigarettes to my mother, but I didn't tell her what happened to me. I knew it wouldn't matter. She never noticed that I was hurt."

There was a terrible silence between my mother and me. I didn't know why, but I hated her clothes - the feel of her underwear, nightgowns and dresses. "When I touched them, I felt dirty," I told Shirley.

A group of alters brought a doll they name "Adele" --Mommy's name -- to the therapy room. They ripped her apart, crushed her head with a toy rolling pin and wanted to cut her up. Shirley gave them scissors and they sliced the doll in a frenzy, throwing the pieces across the floor. "She is empty. She has no heart," they said.

I told Shirley that my mother walked quickly and that my sister and I had to run to keep up with her. "When she shopped downtown, we'd arrive before the store opened. When the alarm clanged she'd plunge forward, my sister and I in her wake. I wonder why she never held our hands?" I asked Shirley.

"She couldn't," Shirley replied.

"I liked it when Mommy was on the phone," said Susie. "She was busy. I'd have fun coloring the flowers on the paper napkins."

"You were the kind of child who could play by herself," Shirley said.

As we talked I remembered my mother's pride in reporting that I was fully toilet-trained by nine months. An image of straps and a potty seat on the toilet flashed into my mind.

"From the time I was a child she laughed at me. According to my sister she laughed at my letter when I wrote to her about being a lesbian and moving to Maine. She laughed again when I asked her about my childhood."

"Only when I had children did she become involved in my life. She enjoyed being a grandmother and has always been very good to my children. When I divorced she didn't speak to me for three years."

I recalled how she would humiliate my sister, and mock my father's mother. "I wanted her to see the therapist with me when I separated from my husband, but she refused."

"You felt she needed professional help," Shirley replied.

"Yes. Maybe I always felt that way."

Daddy's Girl contributed a shocking revelation. "I thought if I was good to Daddy, then Mommy would love me."

Her words reached down to something deep in me, a longing. I remembered shovelling snow to buy knick-knacks and chocolates for my mother. I wanted her love.

"You're talking about what's at the heart of your therapy: being caught between abusive and abandoning parents," Shirley said gently.

One May evening I set out for a walk summoned by the lyrical calls of the tree frogs. Pausing in the meadow I thought about my mother. I'd given up the effort to understand her. If I could simply accept her as she is, with her particular bundle of strengths and weaknesses, that would have to be enough. Would it have been different if she had been able to tell me her story? Would she have loved me if my father hadn't sexually abused me? There were elements in her story and our story together that would never be clear, but on this sweet May evening I felt some resolution.

Turning to old journals I looked for more clues to my history. I was surprised by entries of fifteen years ago. "Sister is out and in control. She's rigid and stuffy. . . . I wish Lynn wouldn't complain about my small voice. I don't know how it happens . . . I don't know if I have a mind." The writing was mine. The words jolted me.

The anxiety didn't abate. "I'm Chair, King, Alex, Hope, and all the rest," Big Barbie announced. "I'm not a separate person. I thought they were different from me; I thought I cared for inner children who were not me. I feel confused and need to rest."

"Pace yourself," Shirley advised. "Get internal support."

Shirley suggested that we create new internal rooms, not organized according to alters, but according to feelings. The alters and I created over a dozen spaces. Big Barbie retired to the place reserved for grieving. But my anxiety remained.

My mind was on fire. I feared the trees crashing through the windows and the floor rising up to crush me. Alters joined with me to control the terror.

"You have a strong imagination," Shirley said.

"That word is too big for us," we replied. We searched inside and heard "the engine world." It felt right.

"The engine world tells us that things will get us and hurt us," we explained. "Sometimes we're in the engine world; sometimes we're in the real world."

"When you were abused, the real world and the engine world got mixed up and you couldn't pull them apart - they were blurred. In the experience of terror, the world is terrifying; everything around you would be frightening."

She went on, speaking thoughtfully. "There were times, perhaps when you were in school and reading a book when it was the real world. At those times, you didn't know about the engine world. But feelings would come and you didn't understand them. They were from the engine world. In the present, there's the real world and the engine world. Both exist," she said.

Naming the engine world gave me and the alters a way to talk about the fears we suffered, as well as the peculiar ideas that intruded on our mind. For example, the alters drew a picture of a baby and thought that the baby was real, or pulled back in fear from a toy male figure, believing that it was real and could hurt them.

I sat quietly on the couch trying to absorb the meaning of all of this. Shirley said,"You have been climbing a mountain for a long time. When you get to the top, you'll know that you're safe. You'll see things. Some things will be good; others, not so good." I drove home imagining the view from the top of that mountain.

SUMMER 1996

> Someone gives me a dozen cards. Broken
> pieces of mirror are glued to them. I
> see a different reflection of myself in each one.
>
> (Dream: June 12, 1996)

On June 1, I joined thousands of other Americans in the Stand for Children march in Washington, D. C. Sixteen buses made the fourteen hour trip from Maine. Watching adults and eager children board the bus brought home the universal hope of a world where children would be loved, safe, and nurtured.

Eilean and I hunkered down in our seats crowding our legs between our stuffed backpacks and bags of food. For eight years we've worked together in many political change efforts. Like others on the bus, we were deeply concerned about the circumstances of children's lives - homelessness, poverty, hunger, disease, physical and sexual abuse - that prevented healthy development. For me the trip was also about reparation. I decided to go not only to bring attention to children and their needs, but to make up in some small way for the harm I've done to children, my own and others. As I grew in understanding of my life experience, I felt more keenly the hurt I had caused.

Riding through the night in the cramped bus I remembered the poor children I had met in Guatemala, Mexico, Nicaragua, and the streets and rutted back roads of urban and rural America. My life was linked with theirs.

The event was an immense Sunday picnic. Children wearing their community tee-shirts walked proudly behind their home-made banners. Children's drawings hung on clothes-lines strung between trees. Some children sang gospel songs; others had their faces painted with flowers.

Prominent speakers called for national legislation that would put children and their needs first on the political agenda. People of different races, ethnic identities, religious beliefs, economic stations and political affiliations stood to applaud this call to action.

I returned to Maine energized by this profound outpouring of hope, commitment, and solid political purpose.

In therapy the alters and I worked together, unless a specific alter needed individual attention. Shirley tried to anchor us in the present. One warm afternoon I told Shirley about images of Daddy near her chair. She stood, quickly moving behind her chair. "I'm in charge. This is my room. Daddy doesn't have that kind of power," she said to me. "This is the present."

In spite of progress, and perhaps because of it, I felt increasingly unstable and agreed to take an anti-depressant medication on a regular basis. Shirley told the child alters about the pill and encouraged them to help the pill do its work.

My dreams steamed with anger. I shouted words of rage and demanded to be heard. "I'm afraid of anger, whether it's my own or others," I confessed to Shirley.

"If a person is afraid of anger and other people know it, then they can't be their full selves with you. You miss the full richness of other people," Shirley replied.

"The next time someone expresses anger, notice if anyone gets hurt. People with post-traumatic stress often tense themselves when someone's angry and when it's over, forget what happened. The cycle repeats itself and nothing changes."

"Sometimes I think of my anger as a whirlpool that spins out of control," I said.

"You either freeze or have a burst of rage," Shirley explained. "We're working for something in-between." Although anger and destruction were linked in my mind, I tucked her words away for further reflection.

My face continued to feel bruised. In therapy, my hands rushed to my face to rub and rub and rub. Shirley pointed out that this was an expression of primary process thinking, that is, using gestures instead of words. "The adult way is to transform feelings into language that describes the feelings. Instead of rubbing your face, you could identify a feeling. We're working toward secondary process thought," she said, "moving away from concrete thinking toward the abstract."

I recalled that Shirley told me earlier that I had a thought disorder, but I was only now beginning to understand how my mind worked.

When my younger daughter arrived for a visit I threw myself into giving her a splendid vacation. We visited the lighthouse at beautiful Quoddy Head, enjoyed a visit to Campobello Island, the summer home of the Roosevelt family, and had fun at an annual rodeo. Our time together was precious and memorable. I wanted to be there for her in ways I wasn't capable of in the past.

The new medication helped and my daily routine was more manageable. But in therapy I unravelled, and released pent up anxiety. "You need a place to do this. You need to let yourself be unglued," Shirley said.

Fragile alters who experienced a distorted reality, like Billy, Alice, Rain and Ruth, were my main concern. Shirley reminded me that they had made gains in therapy, that Billy, for example, changed from disorganized play to wanting to learn to read.

"They have extreme suffering," she said.

"I can't go forward without them; it'd be like building a house on sand."

"You have an unconscious belief that they can't change."

"Maybe their presence confirms that my mind is hurt. Perhaps they remind me of the trauma."

"Survivors have said that the hardest thing to give up is the trauma. What makes you not want them to change?"

"Maybe we're organized around them. We contain and control them. Changing them feels radical."

Silence moved into the room as each of us sat with her own thoughts.

"Would you like to hear how I understand our whole process?" Shirley asked.

"Yes."

"In the beginning you filled up the hour with things you wanted to tell me. I interpreted this as anxiety in the transition to a new therapist. My goal was to say one or two things in a session. Now, I'm able to have a conversation with you. You're more able to look at me. You're more able to let me in on your process, and we work together for insight. I never work harder than you," she observed. "I see you as very committed to your process of healing."

I felt strengthened and thanked her.

In mid-July Myrna and I took a camping trip with Eilean and Sandy. We packed our gear into canoes and paddled across Rocky Lake to an isolated campsite. This pristine lake nestled in the wilderness was glorious. I had only canoed once before, but the simple act of paddling gave me enormous pleasure. My arms and shoulders fell into a rhythm. Everything came together in beauty - my friends, the clear lapping water, towering trees, and the songs of birds.

Alice returned to therapy. "The world is scarey but it's also magic," she declared.

"Who hurt you?" Shirley asked.

The question disturbed Alice and she asked others inside to help her. "I don't know. I never thought of it." Her face filled with sadness. "Daddy. Daddy hurt me. I want to go back inside. Protector will help me," she said.

"She didn't know about Daddy," I said, surprised.

"Alice didn't let herself know about him and the price of that was feeling crazy."

"I feared that she suffered a kind of schizophrenia," I told Shirley.

"I know," she answered softly.

When we met again, Chair emerged. Shirley told her about the before and after worlds. "In the before world, a long, long time ago, you were abused. In the after world that kind of hurting doesn't happen to you."

"How did I get into the after world?" Chair wondered.

"You grew up."

"I see one world over there," Chair said, pointing to one side of the room, "and another in that corner. Maybe there's a tunnel between them."

"The tunnel is time," Shirley answered.

"Can I stay here with you?" Chair exclaimed. "Maybe we could go for walks. I could sleep on the floor. We could play together."

"You feel safe here and want to stay safe but it wouldn't work for you to stay here. We have a special relationship called therapy. I live somewhere else and go home at night."

"I do feel safe here. Hurt is terrible," Chair whimpered.

"Was there ever a time when hurt wasn't part of your experience?" Shirley asked.

"No. In the before world everything is scarey and can get me."

"You were frightened. It wasn't things that hurt you, but people. Would you like to learn about beautiful things in the after world?"

"Oh, yes," shouted Chair.

At home, Jane showed Chair the double buttercup and white peony in the garden; along the shore she helped Chair collect beach stones and sea shells while gulls soared overhead.

During the week Chair thought about the two worlds. She drew a line down the center of her papers. On one side she drew horrible abuse, on the other, flowers and birds. "I'm in the after world now," she said proudly to Shirley.

With Shirley's vacation just a couple of weeks away, I asked if I might take a snapshot of her. She agreed. The picture would remind me of her existence and our relationship. She sat in her chair as she always did while the camera captured her warmth and extreme kindness.

In August, Myrna and I set out for England and Ireland. Like our pilgrimage on Crete, this journey was centered in the Goddess. The experience was blessed. Our travels took us to powerful neolithic stones where the Goddess was likely worshipped and to many Holy Wells where she was remembered and honored. In small and large bottles I gathered water for friends.

At the Famine Museum in Stokestown I deepened my awareness of the depth of suffering endured by the Irish people during the famines. That food was deliberately withheld from the poor was a monumental crime.

In Ireland, I felt deeply at home. Overlooking Galway Bay I entertained Myrna with the familiar Irish tunes of my childhood and stories of classmates who demonstrated the wizardry of step-dancing. In County Sligo we entered the world of Yeats and read his poetry to each other.

I remembered my maternal great grandmother, Annie Sullivan, who was born in Cork. Only one memory of her remains from my childhood. After my grandmother's death, my mother took my sister and me to visit Annie. As my mother sobbed, I heard my great grandmother say, "You were a good daughter to her, Adele." Now, when I looked at her portrait I felt her compassion. It pleased me greatly that we bear a strong resemblance to each other.

AUTUMN 1996

I'm digging into a wall with a pair
of scissors, shouting, "I hate you;
you're mean," over and over.

(Dream: November 29, 1996)

When I visited the tower home of Yeats at Thor Ballylee, I found a beautiful print of one of his poems that described a mind "like still water" in which others "see their own images. . . and so have a fiercer life." I immediately thought of Shirley and bought the print as a gift for her.

Matted and framed, the print was even more compelling. I presented it to Shirley at my first appointment after vacation. "It's beautiful, but I'm not sure I can accept such a big gift." She put it back in the brown shopping bag and placed it beside her desk. "I need to think about this."

"I'll respect your decision," I replied, trying to mask my feelings of shame and humiliation. This difficult beginning made it hard to connect with Shirley and resume therapy.

Aware of my distress she took my hand at the end of the hour. "I'm here for you," she said.

The gift became the axis around which my therapy revolved. "I want us to make this decision together," Shirley said.

I sat with my eyes closed, turned away from her. "You don't want the gift because it reminds you of me. My presents are contaminated because they carry my dirt," I responded.

"I don't feel that way," she said reassuringly. "Tell me about gift-giving in your life."

"I like to give presents to my friends; often they're homemade. As a child, I picked flowers for my teachers and brought home small surprises for my mother, especially knick-knacks which she particularly liked. She'd always say, "All I want is two good girls." An old sadness rose up in me. For a moment I sat quietly. I couldn't give my mother what she wanted.

"How did you feel when your mother said that?" Shirley asked, noting my silence.

"Hopeless," I replied and quickly changed the subject. "Sally and I exchanged small gifts, like flowers, dried herbs, and other things that she or I had made. She enjoyed my gifts and I cherished hers," I explained.

"I'm not comfortable with gift-giving in therapy," Shirley said. "I wish I had clarified this with you earlier."

"When I gave you the knitted socks, I felt you were hesitant. But when I brought you the Goddess figure from Crete you opened it quickly and were obviously pleased. I'm confused."

"I want to give you two compliments," Shirley said. "You're good at gift-giving, and secondly, you're able to address this problem with me right away. Hold open a place inside to keep the process moving."

She sat across from me, large and powerful in the wing-back striped chair. I tried to keep in mind that she was trying to help, but I felt only distrust. As if reading my thoughts she said, "My feelings about you haven't changed. We can work this out."

I slipped into the September night exhausted by the trial of vacillating between blaming Shirley for rejecting me and believing that she was trying to help me. I needed to keep her at a safe distance.

Two days later, we sat opposite each other in the therapy room. "If I simply accept your decision you'll have more power over me; if I don't give in, I'll die."

"Take what you know about your history and link it to these feelings," she said. Daddy filled my mind. Laughing erupted. "Take the feelings of the past and put them in a box," she said. Miraculously, I was able to do this. I looked at Shirley and saw the therapist who was trying to help me. "If I were you," Shirley said, "I might be feeling something like 'Shirley, I never wanted this disruption to happen between us.'"

"Yes. I believe that you deliberately rejected the gift to hurt me and that you get satisfaction from that."

"In the past you rode through these feelings as if riding through a storm and felt relief when it was over. Perhaps we can resolve it in a way that won't make you feel like you're giving in. You don't have the strength to handle negative feelings," she said compassionately.

I knew, rationally, that Shirley was working for my benefit, but emotionally I suspected that she wanted to hurt me. I drew pictures of her - tied up, locked up in a box. I felt murderous and imagined torching her house.

I was surprised by her interpretation of my drawings. "Are you showing me how you feel - powerless, trapped?" she asked, looking at the pictures.

A sadistic alter came forward and talked about being the abused or the abuser. Shirley explained that in the world of abuse one person was higher, the other person was lower. "There is another kind of power, one in which each person respects the other and each has their own feelings. You're saying how you feel and I'm sharing my feelings with you. Both of us have power."

When the alter receded, I squirmed on the couch. "I have been terrified of my own meanness."

"You denied it."

"I didn't want anyone to see it. I buried it and tried to be good. But it makes sense, doesn't it. Why wouldn't I want to hurt others after what happened to me."

"Yes. Your feelings make sense."

Tears filled my eyes. Despite the pain of this conversation I did not feel diminished.

"This is the hardest work you've done with me," Shirley said, referring to the gift. "Thank you for allowing me to do this level of work with you." She was tearful, too.

At home I soothed myself with hot baths and soft oils. I found comfort in brilliant autumn colors. Sitting by the sea I remembered what Shirley said - if something can be, it can change. Perhaps the expression of my fears, hostility, and anger would open to their transformation.

In therapy, associations streamed out unprotected by any alter who might censor them. "My mother said that I was a quiet baby, that I would lie silently on the couch for hours." These words opened to an internal pool of sadness spilling over with fear and despair.

Feelings collided in me. Words caught in my throat. I strained to make sounds. "The first experience was being hurt," I said. "Anyone could lash out to obliterate me; to annihilate me. Despair doesn't adequately describe what I feel. Something like a lament in me," I said anxiously.

Shirley gave a name to the feeling I couldn't express: "Elemental keening," she said. I lay on the couch trying to ease the rapid beating of my heart and my fear of slipping into madness.

The question of the gift remained unresolved. Shirley wondered if I would like to have it back, but I refused. She assured me that we would work this out together. I asked her if she was waiting for me to say or do something.

"No, that's an awful place to be," she replied. "I felt uncomfortable with your gift giving in general, and this present from Ireland escalated my discomfort. It went zooming," she said. I said nothing.

"Don't you want to say,' Sally accepted my gifts. Why won't you?'"

"No. There's no fight in me."

"You want me to make the decision."

"Yes."

"What would it mean to you if I accepted your gift?"

"When someone accepts a gift it's like accepting me," I responded.

"I accept you," Shirley said.

Her words seared into me like a hot knife cutting open an ancient wound. Physical pain shot through my heart, but I also felt healing. "It hurts," I protested, turning away from her. "I feel naked and ashamed. I let you get too close and need to push you away."

"You might feel better if you look at me. If you don't look, you might regret it," she said with care.

"I can't look at you."

"I'll close my eyes and you can open yours." I opened my eyes and I saw her. With her eyes closed, she said, "When I was a little girl I used to run around the house with my eyes closed pretending to be blind. I was afraid of being blind. I'm so glad I'm not because now I can see you."

"You can open your eyes," I told her. I wanted to cry but no tears came.

"You wondered if anyone would accept you. You have shown me so much of yourself since we began to work together, and perhaps in the past few weeks you've been sorry that you've shown me so much."

"Yes. Bad things were done to me. I am bad and did bad things to others."

"I don't see it that way. You're a complex person with a complicated history and that's just fine with me."

After the session I rested in my car, dazed to the bone. I hadn't known the depths of my longing for acceptance. Words had never wounded and healed in this way. An image of a mother bird wrapping a wing around her chick floated into my mind.

Over the next few days I struggled to take comfort in her acceptance, but a gnawing fear got in the way. She reached my center and now I belonged to her. She had power over me.

I stuttered trying to say the words. "Somehow I was ready to let you in to a place which I had protected for a long time. Now I'm in your power and I must do what you want."

"You're choosing to come because you want to heal. I'm not your boss. I don't own you and don't want to. I work for you. You can fire me if you choose."

The dense cloud in my head lifted and I saw clearly that my feelings of being owned were about the past.

My internal world shifted and I noticed stronger feelings toward Shirley. "I feel close to you in a different way. You're not connected to a specific part, but to all of us. This is the first time all of me has been connected," I said excitedly.

Despite this step forward the issue of gift-giving was not settled. Shirley commented that somehow gift-giving, acceptance, and surrender were linked in my mind.

"Daddy gave me away. He surrendered me. I had to surrender. How could he do those things as if I meant nothing?" I lay on the couch, laughing, gripping the pillow. "Appeasement - gifts are about appeasing, hoping nothing bad will happen."

"Yes," Shirley said softly.

I wanted to shake her, make her do something. Quickly I realized that these feelings were about my father. I wanted and needed his help. He offered none.

At my desk I wrote about patterns of surrender in my life - with my father, in relationships, in work. Sadly I recognized that I sometimes felt a certain odd pleasure in surrendering.

I told Shirley about the fear that gripped me when she looked at me, "If I look at you it'll be a surrender; if I don't look, then I don't connect."

"Either you resist or surrender," she observed. "Try to give words to these feelings. What if you say, I need to break contact with you." Her words generated a new clarity. I hadn't realized that my actions were a replacement for words. Now I was beginning to understand what Shirley meant by primary process thinking: I act things out much as a child would because I didn't have the words. Finding emotional language would help me move into the abstraction and logic of secondary process thought.

The failing light of October was brightened by Molly and Maeve, two calico kittens, sisters, who came to live with us. Their playfulness charmed me. I lay on the rug rolling balls of yarn and watched them scamper in great delight. Their sweet purring and deep sleep on our laps were abundance. The four of us formed ardent bonds.

Finally, in early November Shirley said that it would be unethical for her to take the gift. "I want you to have a relationship in which you don't give gifts. You don't have to give me any gifts. Our relationship feels more equal if you don't give gifts." She suggested that perhaps I would like to make a donation of it somewhere.

"I feel like I've transgressed. But I wouldn't want you to feel uncomfortable," I said sadly.

A week later Shirley left the gift, still in the brown paper bag, outside her office. I took it home and hung it in my study. This gift for her had become an amazing gift for me - one that had cut into and through the pain of my heart. I heard her words, "I accept you."

WINTER 1996-1997

I'm in the country with a group of people.
Ahead of us is an immense mountain dense
with trees. I can't imagine getting over it.
Someone says, "All the land was like that at
first."

(Dream: February 14, 1997)

I was no longer afraid of my father or other perpetrators. Instead, I became afraid of my mind and my terrifying emotions. Shirley reminded me that I had learned to hold myself together and endure the feelings, waiting for them to pass.

"Your feelings have something to offer you; they're a flow of energy in the present, indicators that something happened to you. Imagine going down a river on a raft and when you see the rapids you close your eyes and hang on; or imagine that you look at the rapids, hold onto the raft and move with the rapids. You'd feel excitement and mastery. It's important for you to learn how to move with your feelings," she said.

"I fear that my feelings can kill me."

"Yes, but they never have. Before you had words you had these feelings. Now you are finding words for them. Suppose you think of them as friendly, like an ever-changing river flowing in ripples, in rapids, and in smooth currents. You will learn to ride the waves."

Shovelling snow the next day, I pondered her words. The snow was wet and heavy. I worked carefully, sensitive to my back. I had believed that the feelings came either from the alters or seized me from outside, that I was a victim of my feelings. If they were mine in the present, perhaps I could learn from them. Perhaps I could even befriend them.

Back in therapy, Shirley told me another story. "Suppose I look out the window and see a tree against the night sky. I experience a pleasure which goes back to my childhood when I sat on my porch in the dark and looked at the trees. The pleasure goes back in my life but it is also real in the present. Having feelings is the difference between a sketch and a rich oil painting."

I held a pillow in my lap, fingering the soft rose fabric. Outside, the light of day disappeared. I recalled painful moments when people asked about my feelings and I had nothing to say. My feelings were hidden from me until Sally rolled back the stone. I wondered how I would have experienced feelings in a natural way - without the imposition of trauma.

Therapy was shifting more decidedly toward integration as present emotion replaced the focus on past trauma. "The future creates a different past," Shirley told me. "Out of the trauma, you became a woman with compassion for people who suffer. The point is not to forget the past, but to integrate it." She told me about children who have been kidnapped. "When they are rescued, the children are encouraged to tell what happened until they have no further need to tell. In the end they describe how it feels to have kidnapping as part of their history." This story clarified what I needed to do for myself.

In early winter I succumbed to the flu. When the male doctor looked into my throat and ears I was overcome with the feeling of being filthy, repulsive. The doctor became my father exploring my body. He talked to me but I couldn't hear him. I slid from the examining table and found refuge in a bathroom.

"You were taken by surprise," Shirley said. "Perhaps it would be helpful to identify the reactions as post-traumatic responses. Honor the feeling and explore it when you have time. This may help you stay in the present."

"Is there something else wrong with me?" I asked.

"Before the nature of trauma was understood, many women were diagnosed with schizophrenia. When therapists identified post-traumatic stress disorder and dissociation, a conceptual change took place. Now we are looking again. The lines between schizophrenia and dissociation are blurred," she explained. "You have symptoms of schizophrenia."

"What do you mean?"

"You have a thought disorder and mini-psychotic episodes. When you were a child, you had a choice between dissociating or going crazy. Sometimes the dissociation didn't work and you lost your mind. You know about feeling crazy from your own experience. We are forming a story that honors all of your history. As we work, your mental health will improve; you'll gain insight and learn to manage the symptoms. You have more choices than going crazy."

I said nothing, but the word "schizophrenia" felt like a boulder in my mind. The dreaded fear of collapsing into such a complete retreat from reality terrified me, but somewhere in me, I knew that Shirley was right in naming these symptoms. The fur and claws that grew on my hands and the experience of being dismembered were only two of the unrealities which for me were real.

Shirley saw my internal world and reflected it back to me. Walking out into the cold December night I felt protected by her understanding.

On the third day of Christmas Myrna and I made love for the first time in seven years. My desire for her had finally eclipsed the fear that kept me distant. The past did not intrude into this wondrous moment. Our touching wove a love that brought us home to one another.

In therapy Shirley and I continued the process of integration. I asked Shirley about therapists who suggested that it was better to remain multiple, that integration was somehow a choice to be conventional. Shirley said, "Some people who feel centered in their lives may say that multiples have more options because they're less confined. They say it because they have a centered life and don't know what it's like to live with multiplicity."

Her words freed me from the fear of "doing it wrong." I chose again to be an integrated woman.

Chair, Alice, and Ruth re-emerged. They sat in the play corner, piling blocks in a great heap. Seeing a Bambi toy, they remembered the little fawn fleeing the forest fire. "If you close your eyes, then nothing happens," they exclaimed to Shirley.

"You have a kind of mystery time. When you're ready, you can learn what happened in that time," she replied.

I returned. My fingers moved over my hands and my feet sank into the carpet to assure myself of existence. Shirley said, "Chair and others closed their eyes to cope with trauma, but when they opened them they didn't know what had happened. They only had feelings of terror. If they can remember the trauma, they'll be able to attach their feelings to something real." This made good sense to me and explained the powerful disorientation they experienced.

Protector suggested that it would be better for them to grow up before they remembered the trauma. They liked this idea and recruited others inside to help them. Spreading a group of toy figures in front of Shirley's chair they began their story. "Now we are five years old and can trace Old King Cole on the linoleum. At eight we have strong arms and can play Red Rover. At ten we see monkeys, elephants and giraffes at the zoo. At twelve we ride the subway and stand in front of the grate to feel the wind. At fourteen we roller skate in an indoor rink. At sixteen we wear lipstick and fix our hair."

"You've come a long way," said Shirley encouragingly. Chair, Alice, and Ruth liked being sixteen. "We feel strong and can do more things." They looked at the dolls resting against the wall and chose a koala bear. "There's no heartbeat; the ears and mouth are sewn shut."

"Children often think that things are real when they aren't. It's a loss to discover that things aren't the way they imagined them to be. Perhaps it's important for you to think the dolls are real," Shirley mused.

"Yes. The dolls look at us; they see us and hear us. They're our friends. If they're not real, then we're all alone. The dolls won't hurt us, won't call us names."

"You know what they're going to say, but you don't know what I'll say. I can imagine what baby is feeling as she rests in her crib, but these are my thoughts."

The group looked quizzically at Shirley and returned inside.

My bizarre laugh filled the room. "I still don't feel the abuse happened to me," I confessed. "Until I feel it, it isn't mine."

"Sometimes in fighting a fire, the firefighters will build another blaze to fend off the more dangerous one. But they still have to overcome the first fire. Your scarey world is like a second fire."

I worked at closing the distance between the alters and me. Using Shirley's phrasing, I repeated," Sometimes I felt sexy. Sometimes I felt destructive. Sometimes I had murderous thoughts. Sometimes I felt terrified. Sometimes I move into a space where I can teach a class. Sometimes I move into a space where I can be clinically useful to another person." The words rolled out linking me with the experience of the alters and my own diverse possibilities.

"Can you say, 'I sometimes have feelings of excitement in response to violence?'" Shirley suggested.

"No. Those feelings are sadistic, evil, monstrous. If I say those words, the feelings might grow. "

"I did not have the experience you have had; I'm not excited by violence. But imagine that I told you that I was emotionally excited by violence and that I learned those feelings because I was brought into an environment where violence and excitement meshed. What if I told you that I struggled with those feelings, that I had to work through shame to be able to talk about them. You would be compassionate and say how hard that must be, how terrible."

"Yes. I would not blame, criticize, or judge you."

"You were brought into a culture that was excited by violence. When you were able, you chose to do good things."

"What is real in me: peace or sadism?"

"Both are real. Everyone has loving and destructive feelings," she answered.

Her words fell into me. They attached to those internal places where I feared my power. A new understanding of wholeness - of goodness and evil - was trying to take deeper root in me.

SPRING 1997

> I'm in Sally's house. She died but is now
> alive for three days. She holds my face and
> blows gently. I open my mouth and she breathes
> into me, giving me her spirit.
>
> (Dream: March 21, 1997)

On the second anniversary of Sally's death, Shirley and I read together the prayer to the Great Mother Kunapipi, the one Sally chose for her memorial. I was awash with memories of Sally. I honored her emotional bravery with me and her physical fortitude facing the armed military in El Salvador. In my dreams she was both living and dead. We would always be connected to each other.

In early March, Shirley challenged my separateness from the alters. "The alters seem to be leaving therapy to you. They disclose their memories but there still remains a wall between you." She wondered if any part of us felt that she was pushing integration.

Images of the cult swirled through my mind and intense laughing filled the room. "Some of us don't want to integrate the alters involved with the cult," I said adamantly.

"Are the cult alters listening? I wonder what it would mean to them to be accepted. Is there someone who could speak for the group?" Shirley queried.

"It would mean that the others accepted our feelings and experiences," Margie said, emerging and retreating quickly.

My mind wandered. To accept the reality of the cult was repulsive to me. I knew that memory is not entirely reliable and that a mind is not a video camera. Perhaps the memories of the cult were symbolic; perhaps they were confused stories of my internal life, rather than external realities.

"Do you suppose the alters have confused Catholic rituals with the trauma?" I asked.

"You want me to interpret the cult away," Shirley said knowingly.

"Yes. I don't want it in my life. After Sally left I never wanted to mention it again. But feelings, thoughts, and images of the cult won't let go."

"You need to tell the story of the cult as an adult."

Outside of therapy I was determined to think about other matters. A group of friends joined with me to plan a retirement party for Myrna. We wanted it to be spectacular. Our meetings were hilarious as we worked out skits, music, costumes, and props for a review of Myrna's life. We rented a hall and I busied myself with long lists of food, invitations, and decorations. Myrna knew about it, but the details remained secret. She and Diane, the Mistress of Ceremonies, rented tuxedos for the gala, and plans moved ahead with great anticipation.

In quiet moments I discussed cult alters with other internal members. We reached a decision to accept their stories as interpretations of their experience, a kind of emotional truth. Feeling relieved we presented this achievement to Shirley.

"Are all of you accepting it as your emotional truth?" she asked.

Her question surprised me. Many alters had no relation to the cult. Sister burst into the room. "The cult is sinful, dirty, evil; I don't want anything to do with it."

"You're at a decision point. Would you accept a transformation of your identity by integrating those parts which you fear, or do you want to remain separate?" Shirley asked.

Sister clasped her hands. "I want to be good. I hate anything connected to Satan." Her hands suddenly moved to her face, registering shock. "If I shut out those alters abused by the cult, that's rejection," she said slowly and deliberately.

"God could have simply bestowed blessings and stayed apart from the world, but He became man in Jesus and made humanity part of Him," Shirley offered. "I'm invested in being good, too, and it's hard to accept that I can be mean and petty at times. You've wanted to be good but no one is perfect."

Sister leaned toward Shirley. "I never thought of it like that before. I didn't imagine that aspiring to goodness would mean accepting the cult alters, and that rejection of them would be less than good. I feel a reconciliation inside, but now I need to rest."

I felt stirred by Sister's efforts. At the end of the session I grasped Shirley's hands. I asked her to pray for me. "I don't think I'll make it."

She held my hands in both of hers. "I'll pray for you. You're afraid of being crazy."

"Yes."

"You've constructed a good life that you're heading into," she said with encouragement.

In the sessions that followed, alters that had emerged after my childhood absorbed the experience of cult alters. I was finally able to say," We accept them as they are. Everything they report doesn't have to be objective truth. They are us and we are them." I spoke quietly and with immense relief. But when I looked across the room at Shirley my vision was blurred.

"You've done a lot of work. You're feeling an overload," she said empathically.

All of us agreed to write the story of the cult and read it to Shirley. The pain of giving words to the terror made me rub my body and laugh uncontrollably. When I finally read the story to her, I rushed to the conclusion and exclaimed, "The End."

"There aren't words enough for this," I cried. "Horrible, violent, cruel, sadistic don't describe it. Why did Daddy do this to us? We felt so powerless. We were beyond fear. Nothing was left inside. It was hard being a little girl who had died. We were made of straw. Alone. Things were unreal. Nothing mattered. We couldn't give or receive love. We couldn't tell anybody that we were made of straw."

"It's all over now. You're big. It won't happen again," Shirley said with tears in her eyes. "How do you feel about the work you've done?"

"In our heart of hearts we knew we had to do this. We had to face the violence, the emptiness, the straw."

At home, Myrna observed that I appeared dazed, but I couldn't speak. I shuddered at the losses in my life. My thoughts turned to bewildering experiences in graduate school. There were times when my mind wouldn't work, when lectures and readings made no sense; times when I found information muddled and unfathomable; times when memorizing was the only option. I remembered that sad rainy day when I carried a large plastic bag with every book I was studying to a meeting with my advisor. He gently expressed concern for me and offered lunch. Perhaps he could see that my behavior and thinking were chaotic and disorganized.

Shirley listened to these and other episodes and said, "You had no perspective on yourself."

My instability continued with feelings that were ungrounded and dreams that were filled with destruction. Shirley taught me to place my hands on my lower abdomen and repeat, "It is true that in the greater part of my life I am safe and have no need to fear, and it is also true that there are times that are frightening and fear is a response." The practice soothed me as I opened to deeper feelings about my history.

Shirley reminded me that "Many of the alters have talked about their feelings, but it's important that they work them through." In the coming weeks I listened as Ruth and Alice achieved a clearer grasp of reality, and King and Not Barbara transformed their roles in the system. For my part, I learned to respond to difficult feelings by checking inside to discover who was in distress and what they might need.

One evening I felt fur and claws growing out of my hands. I thought it was really happening and felt afraid and disoriented. Checking inside, I learned that an alter was remembering a painful trauma. Fur and claws protected me from remembering.

Shirley listened. "Until now it has been important to you to have the symptom instead of letting yourself know what happened. The feelings of fur and claws obscure the trauma."

"Yes. I'm so afraid of losing my mind, of not knowing who I am, or of being uncontrollably angry; but I want to know what I know."

In mid-May, Myrna was Grand Marshal at the college graduation. Her face glowed as she walked elegantly down the aisle. At the reception she was further honored for her many contributions to college life, especially her mentoring of women students and the introduction of women's studies and multiculturalism into the curriculum.

On the evening of her party, she was dazzling in her tuxedo. We walked into the glittering hall to the sounds of "Stepping Out"; we glided into dance, feeling love for each other and for our beautiful community of friends. The night was magic.

SUMMER 1997

> A group of us want to get through a narrow passageway, but the door is barred and nailed shut.
>
> (Dream: July 23, 1997)

In early June, I joined with members of my family to celebrate the birth of David and Tina's infant daughter. Old persistent feelings of being an outsider plagued me. I was a mother whose mental illness diminished my capacity to parent; I was also a lesbian. Still, I felt blessed when I observed my grown children talking and laughing with one another. When I held my grandaughter, my heart swelled.

Sitting in a cafeteria, my sister and I tried to speak truths to each other. "I've never known how to be close," Jody said. "I know that there's a disturbance in me. I've never belonged anywhere. I fake sanity. I have thoughts and images about being violent toward others." I listened, noting how alike we were.

She continued, "Mom always laughed at us. She was sarcastic and mocking, but I think she did the best she could." The pain in her confession clouded her eyes.

Then she pulled from her handbag a set of flyers which advertised her work. I looked over the papers and thought of how, in the sphere of work, her talent and passionate spirit brought her success. I felt deep love for her.

I was taken by surprise the morning that Shirley said that she felt uncomfortable with our handshaking at the close of our sessions. "What are your feelings about this?" she asked.

"Shaking hands seems to make our relationship more solid. It's a way to express my appreciation."

"I don't want anything covert between us - something there but unspoken."

I turned away from her. "I feel ashamed that I've transgressed."

"I understand your feelings, but you haven't transgressed."

"I feel dirty, contaminated."

"That's your stuff," I heard Shirley say. I floated far away. Her voice was like distant muffled sound.

Shirley continued, "I'm trying to maintain a connection between us. Is Not Barbara here?"

Not Barbara sat sullenly. "There's no one else. The others are hiding."

"You weren't even involved in this. How do you feel handling this alone?" Shirley asked.

Not Barbara walked out. Ten minutes later I returned to the office having resumed control. "I should be able to handle this. You were uncomfortable. I won't do it again."

"Can you look at me, Barbara?" My eyes remain closed. "If you leave without looking you'll have a distortion instead of me as I am." I didn't respond.

"I don't want to fake it with you. I like you. I want integrity in our relationship. I'll close my eyes and turn my head so you can look at me," she said, moving as she spoke. I paused, then opened my eyes. There was something sad in seeing her turned away from me.

Four days later I was back in her office. I considered cancelling but I knew I needed to deal with her. "Are you interested in knowing why I felt uncomfortable?" she asked.

"No. I don't trust you. I'm afraid that it'll hurt us."

"It might. It's hard for me to be with you like this."

"I feel betrayed. The rules were changed in mid-stream."

"Perhaps you were hoping that this kind of thing wouldn't happen in our relationship. Do you feel tension in our relationship?"

"No. You're like my mother. She hated my body."

"This is about transference. Do you know what I mean?"

"Yes, I attribute to you feelings that I had about my mother. But I know you're not my mother."

"It's a negative transference," Shirley said.

"I know that you've helped us. We were even able to work through the problem with the print from Ireland."

"That gives you hope," Shirley replied. "I appreciate that you've opened your eyes and are looking at me. It's hard to be with someone who sits with closed eyes not looking at me. You're saying, 'Fuck you, Shirley.'"

"I never said that."

"Your behavior said that. In any intimate relationship there are problems. Learning to work them out is part of therapy. What I said hurt you very deeply. And now you hurt me. I'm hurt by your behavior."

"You seem to feel that your hurt is equal to mine," I said angrily.

"No. Do you want to hear how I felt about the handshaking?" I shook my head.

"I respect that, but at some time we'll have to deal with it. You think that by complying with a rule this will be over - that you will comply and endure. Is that familiar?"

"Yes."

But I knew it wasn't over. I dwelt on the problem. A chorus of voices clamored from within. A week later I sat opposite her apologizing for my bad behavior. "Part of my anger is toward myself. I shouldn't have reached out for a handshake, to let that need be known."

"Initially when we shook hands it seemed to emerge naturally from a celebratory experience, a feeling of exuberance that we both shared. Then it happened more often and I sensed that you were expressing a need. I feel that it's more therapeutic to talk about needs than to satisfy them. Acting them out is a painkiller that temporarily dulls pain but doesn't go to the source. The last time we shook hands I felt something off and that's why I brought up my concerns. I'm sorry. I made a mistake. My practice is to have no physical contact. Inadvertently, I set you up. I'm truly sorry."

"I'm trying to accept your apology." My eyes closed in response to powerful contradictory feelings: isolation, anger, fear. Shirley's voice seemed low and remote. When I opened my eyes I was surprised that she was there.

"When you close your eyes we are both without bodies," she explained. I left the session exhausted, thinking only of sleep.

I was relieved to throw myself into other things. Myrna and I celebrated the summer birthdays of friends, plunged our hands into garden soil, and hosted a party to thank our friends for the retirement gifts that made our new deck possible. Marlene and I went to her granddaughters' dance recital. As I watched the little girls tap across the stage I was transported back to the Gertrude Dolan studio in 1945 where Jody and I learned shuffle-ball change, cartwheels, and ballet. For years a picture of us in dancing costumes sat on the living room table. A voice from within said, "I know how to tap dance, too."

I returned to therapy and found a typed letter from Shirley folded on the couch. She described physical patterns that express a courageous, self-possessed state: eyes open, breathing full, relaxed upright posture, whether standing or sitting. Her note also contained two quotes about trust in relationship. Although the evidence that she thought of me was comforting, discouragement stuck to my bones.

"How are you feeling about our relationship?" she asked.

"I think of you as a doctor I visit. You seem distant. I miss the warmth in our relationship."

"You seem to want to protect yourself."

"Yes. I'm afraid of you. I don't like talking about our relationship because I'm afraid I'll make a mess."

"This change feels like a loss. Maybe you took me in and idealized me and then you found out that I was just me, your therapist. That would feel like a loss."

"I don't know, but this pattern is familiar. I retreat, and resist emotional engagement."

"You got to a place that you felt enough trust to continue therapy and work with me. I feel very engaged with you. You are looking at me. I'm not blocked out."

"Yes, but I fear that you'll think I want more than you are willing to give me."

"I know that this is hard for you but I think that there is something more here that will help you with your life."

Her words invited more exploration. I walked the beach on a sky-blue day feeling the absence of mother-love in my life. Molly, our precious cat, followed and curled in my lap as I rested against a rock. I thought about the handshake, about the maternal warmth I felt, and of Shirley's approving smile.

When I divulged these confusing thoughts about mother-love to Shirley, she replied, "I can't provide mother-love to you, nor do I want to. It would hold you back from the next step in therapy."

"I'm grown up. I don't need a mother," I said, but my insides were clamoring and I felt like a lost child. Words spewed from me as my body rocked back and forth. "Without a mother there's no child. Without a mother I wouldn't exist." My words shocked me into silence.

"You're touching on an old belief: if you let go of your need for a mother you wouldn't exist. Until now, you've believed that without mother-love you'd die or go crazy."

I was stunned by the insight.

"You've gone through therapy as a child. The warmth in our relationship isn't about maternal love. The goal of therapy is to grow up and leave. We have warmth in other ways in our work and we'll have it again."

Her words seemed to criticize me and I retorted, "You're kicking me when I'm down. You're trying to control me."

"You're pissed and it's okay," she said. "I've been rough on you." She seemed to be mocking me and my anger escalated.

"You want it all your way. You say, 'Let there be wholeness,' and there is." I bounded out the door, but within an hour left words of apology on her message machine.

At the next session, I felt repentant when she looked at me across the therapy room. "I'm sorry about the way I talked to you. I felt so disconnected."

"My take is different," Shirley said "I felt energy in you. We were really engaged. Not all of it was nice, but there was a real give and take. I was feeling a fondness for you. I want you to know that I'm with you in this process. It was hard but we stayed with it."

"I still feel I need to protect myself, but I believe that you're working to help me. If we changed our relationship I felt there'd be nothing. If I let go of my hope for a loving mother I would have only the void or connection with terrible abuse." My fingers scratched my chest; I repeated the words over and over.

"You think that is the only option," Shirley said.

"Yes, I don't want you to be the abusive daddy," I confided.

My body sank into the couch, relaxed by a new awareness. In the handshake I felt love. When she withdrew, there was the void. I feared going forward because abuse was inevitable. Emotional pieces seemed to fall into place. When I returned to therapy, I groped for ways to express tangled feelings.

"Someone is cutting me up. I see myself being dismembered. Being cut up is Daddy abusing me. Hurting me. His big penis. He was so big. Everytime he hurt us a part of us would go out and suffer the experience for the rest of us. He took so many parts of us and gave parts of us to others. Mommy took parts of us. Jeannie, Hope, Mimi, Mary and so many others held the pain. But there were parts of us that stayed safe. Big Barbie, Peril, Protector, and the whole second system created a safe place inside where Daddy could not reach. We couldn't let Daddy have all of us. We wanted to keep ourselves. We could only stay safe by giving away parts of us. There were times when it was almost impossible to hold on. It was so hard to stay safe."

Tears cleansed my face. Shirley waited quietly. My words continued slowly, deliberately. My right hand covered my heart. "This is the place where they stayed safe. God and Jesus stayed with them. Shock waves cracked the safe place. Peril stood in the crack, knowing both the safe and unsafe place. When the abuse stopped, sprouts began to grow from parts which were safe. They did things in the world, not knowing what happened to them, and not understanding their fear and sadness. Then they met Sally.

She understood them. After she left, Shirley listened. Everyone inside helped each other. I feel such gratitude for the ones who held on. They are blessed."

"Do they feel blessed?" Shirley asked.

"Yes," they said.

I lay exhausted on the couch for a few minutes, then slowly sat up.

"There's something I want to say. I want to say it with my eyes opened, looking at you, Shirley. I is all of us. Me is all of us. I know who I am. I feel alive in my life. I have a life."

"The parts that stayed safe gave you a home to return to," Shirley said softly.

"I never imagined this. I've survived a kind of madness. I feel precious to myself. I want to be gentle to myself. The problem with the handshake helped me get to this place. Thank you, thank you."

Shirley smiled. We sat for a while in the silence.

"Grace abounds," I said.

"Yes," she repeated. "Grace abounds."

AUTUMN 1997

On my way to see Shirley my car changes
shape. The roads change shape. I don't know where
I am and I have no control.

(Dream: November 20, 1997)

My pleasure in achieving integration dominated my life. Myrna cried when I told her and we held each other. In other relationships, too, I felt more emotionally stable and personally confident. My fear of saying peculiar things or acting inappropriately significantly diminished. "I wonder about checking in to see if all parts are integrated," Shirley asked the next week.

The worst happened. Rocking, laughing, clapping my hands. The energy was intense. My body felt dismembered.

"Is it Barbara who's having this experience?" Shirley questioned. "It's me and it's also not me." I placed my hands on my abdomen, feeling my breath move in and out.

"How would you describe your feelings when you're in this state?" Shirley asked.

"Disoriented. Crazy."

"Ungrounded," she added.

"Yes, that's the best word.

"When a child's in a state of chronic trauma with no way to make sense of her environment, she'll feel crazy. We'll need to explore the feeling that you have about being crazy. Keep in mind that it's an occasional feeling in your life, not all of the time."

I knew that her question about whether some alters were not yet integrated triggered this response. Alters that I may not know yet predictably threw me into chaos.

As if reading my thoughts Shirley reminded me that work with known alters had led to healing and growth. She urged me to relax and counted to five. Then I heard another voice.

"There are five of us but I speak for them. You can call me Penny. I have five toes on each foot. I never went to school. You scare me," she said, looking at Shirley.

I heard Shirley review the safety rules and suggest that Penny sleep until they could do more work. On the count of five Penny drifted off and I returned. I felt disappointment, loss, even some shame. I had forgotten that the therapeutic process is not linear but a spiral of inching forward, falling backward, and moving forward again.

"It's important to make room for your disappointment," Shirley said empathically. "It's okay to be in parts to do your work. Penny made progress. She was able to talk, to listen, to identify feelings. Perhaps you could suggest peaceful dreams to her. How are you feeling?"

"Therapy will help her; I'm not so afraid," I replied.

Over the next few meetings Penny opened her world. She built and knocked down blocks, moved everything out of the dollhouse to keep it safe, and hid the baby doll under layers of wrapping. After Shirley reassured her that Daddy was dead and that his friends were likely dead or very far away, Penny placed dolls around a table and began to describe a sadistic ritual.

"I kept asking Protector to help," Penny whimpered.

"When you were reaching for Protector she couldn't help you. She was a little girl like you. Maybe you'd like to check inside and find out yourself," Shirley said.

"Wow," Penny shouted on her return. "They said that we're all fifty-six years old. What happened to me?"

"You grew up and didn't know it. Someday you'll feel grown up and know how to protect yourself," Shirley explained.

After the session I drove to the lake and breathed in the cool September air. Hints of change glimmered in the leaves overhead. I wanted no more alters; no more talk of the cult. At the water's edge I touched beautiful rocks, turning them over in my hands. I felt a subtle internal shift and knew that the integration was not holding.

Shirley wasn't surprised. "Perhaps you might have an internal meeting to discuss partial integration; you could then continue to work this way with the new alter." We gathered for a conversation and agreed to join together.

Despite this resolution, therapy moved down a different track. I was repulsed by Penny's disclosures about the cult: the depravity, inhumanity, pain; the convergence of sex, pleasure, and violence. I didn't want this to be part of my history.

"I recognized my attraction to pain in the convent," I told Shirley. "When I kissed the floor, wore the chain on my arm, or prostrated myself, I felt an odd pleasure."

"The return of the repressed," Shirley commented.

"I remember doing spiritual rituals when I lived alone. The intense feelings were disturbing. Now I wonder if I was unconsciously trying to work something out. I felt my spirituality was fake; I was afraid of it. Now I wonder if those feelings were related to the cult." I never made these connections before and as I spoke I felt something clearing in me.

"I never explored the spiritual aspects of the cult. They did get into my soul. When people say that I'm a spiritual person, I deflect their words. Now I see that I linked my spirituality with evil."

Shirley encouraged me to look at her, to stay in the present.

"No wonder I couldn't take religious vows. Many alters felt they belonged to the cult." I lay on the couch. Weird laughter spun out and feelings of dissolution overwhelmed my body.

"Check inside to see if it's important to explore those feelings now," Shirley said.

I opened my eyes. Shirley was my father. The doors were openings in the room through which dangerous people could enter.

"Get in touch with those parts of yourself who know who I really am," she suggested. I struggled to accept the knolwedge that she was Shirley and finally succeeded.

"You've done excellent work," she said. "In the past, alters would emerge, disclose their trauma, and return inside. This time, you are working with the feelings. If they can be, they can change."

In late September my younger daughter, Ellen, called from Virginia to say that she was moving to Maine. My excitement was unbridled. Myrna and I swung into motion to search for an apartment. I spent early mornings rummaging through stored boxes for useful household supplies and swooped down on local sales with great determination. By the time she and her dog arrived, a cozy apartment was waiting for them. Our happiness spilled over in this blessed new beginning.

Shirley reminded me about our decision of partial integration and wondered what kept us from moving in that direction. After some discussion Peril admitted that "faced with a new group of alters we believed we were stronger if we were separated. That's what helped us survive."

But it didn't take long now for the alters to recognize that the present was different from the past and that division was no longer necessary.

I was eager to integrate, even partially. "Big Barbie and I will be able to soothe the ones inside," I told Shirley.

"Try talking about it differently," Shirley urged. "Instead of saying that Big Barbie will soothe, say that you have the ability to soothe yourself as a mother would." She reminded me that many alters offered comfort in different ways: Jane drew from nature; Barbara Davis turned to faith; Jeannie energized herself through play.

"When I look back I see these capacities in my life."

"But you didn't feel them as your own," Shirley added.

We were ready to integrate and chose the image of the rainbow. Penny's group was invited to watch. We closed our eyes, imagining all the hues, shades, and tones. Shirley guided the process, speaking softly:". . . a place for every hue, feeling how every shade blends into the other, forming a whole. . . . "

We felt ourselves moving together like the colors of the rainbow. Oneness deepened. My eyes opened, brimming with tears. I felt such thankfulness. "I'm a person, connected in myself, connected to everything else." My tears spilled over.

Shirley raised her right hand, "Yeah."

My younger son arrived for a visit in October. Steve waited outside the airport with open arms. How I love this young man! We toured through Down East Maine sharing our souls in hours of conversation. I watched him walk the beach and photograph unusual images.

He, Myrna, and I drove to Quebec and sauntered through the streets and churches of the quaint Old City. The morning was fun until we were lost and I couldn't understand the map. Steve and Myrna laughed, but my frustration burst out. He held my hands and urged me to breathe. I followed his instructions but still felt upset. He told me that I didn't try hard enough. He was right. I tried again and was able to relax. Later, Steve said that he was glad it happened as it validated some childhood memories when I would unexpectedly lash out. I apologized profusely.

Our time together was rich in attachment. When he departed for California, I missed him deeply.

Being with my son and daughter evoked painful experiences from the past. I poured out my grief to Shirley. "Who's talking to me?" she asked.

"I'm Barbara but I feel very different from the Barbara who teaches. I'm not an adult but I'm one person."

"You seem to know it on a theoretical level. You seem somewhere between integration and division. You need more experience as a whole person living in the present."

"I'm trying hard. I'm using the image of the rainbow to strengthen the integration." I paused. I reminded myself that my hands were real to keep from dissolving.

"I know my anxiety is somehow related to not allowing myself to feel my feelings. Something blocks those feelings. I wonder how people experience deep rage, grief, or joy. Maybe I don't feel the emotions because my experience isn't real. I don't acknowledge it as real. If I acknowledged my experiences as real I wouldn't survive."

"Say that again, Barbara," Shirley said. I repeated the words.

"You have a core belief that if you acknowledged the abuse as real you wouldn't survive. Part of you accepts the abuse as real but part of you denies it is."

"But I'm here. I've survived it physically, but not mentally or emotionally. There are times when I feel more stable accepting it as real." I returned to my feeling of being different from other people. I still wondered if what I suffered stemmed from trauma or something else.

"You've lived with mental illness all your life and that may contribute to your sense of difference. It also may be social anxiety and shyness. You do have some signs of schizophrenia: blurry vision, primary process thinking, hallucinations. We work with a group of alters until they are oriented and feel better. Then, there's another group. One explanation is that they're groups of alters who can be treated as dissociated parts of yourself. Another explanation is that you have a strand of schizophrenia which takes the form of alters and continues to come out in these ways."

I thought about that gray area where schizophrenia and dissociation overlapped. When trauma overwhelmed the dissociative defenses, my mind was hurt and I developed a thought disorder. I feared the broken place in me where my mind was lost.

Although I tried to remember and practice the methods of anxiety reduction Shirley had taught me, I felt little control over some feelings. I focused on her statement that we were trying to create a space between an event and my reaction. The work was hard.

One November morning Shirley suggested that I sit in a different chair in the therapy room. She wondered if it would help me stay in the present as an adult. I moved to the red chair, but it felt too high. I chose her winged-back chair, the chair that Sally also sat in. For a few moments I sat quietly, remembering.

"I'm afraid to talk about things that might trigger me."

"You can remind yourself that you can have your self. You can have your feelings and you can talk about your feelings - your feelings are from your history - you can also say that you're not ready to talk of some things now. You're talking about your life and experiences as a whole person and this is new ground."

In the next therapy hour I couldn't stop laughing. Shirley wondered if it was a sign of trauma not yet integrated. I tried to tell a memory of abuse while remaining in my adult self. In a moment I was lost and returned to my breath to ground myself.

"Is talking directly about an experience different from the feelings you have had after an alter has described an experience?"

"Yes. The colors are more vivid. The event is intense. I see a fuller picture - the building, the steps, and the room."

"This is about post-traumatic stress disorder. When you tell the story you feel it is now."

"Yes. I become lost in that moment - no sense of my body, no sense of time."

"Dissociation in the context of fear and trauma involves primary process thinking. You become lost in the feeling, disconnected from thinking. What we are doing is working to integrate your trauma into secondary process thought. It would be helpful to bring more of your daily life into therapy. We need to make a solid cognitive foundation in order to integrate the trauma."

I was frightened by Shirley's black pants. "Come, look at them. See the seam and the hem. They are my pants. Check out reality. This is a way to stay in the present." I touched the soft corduroy and my fears slipped away. I wondered what might keep me in the present with the resources of my full adult self. Thinking of Speaker, I suggested pen and paper.

Shirley went to her desk and brought them to me. I felt myself evolving into an adult identity. I made a mental note to include pen and paper as fixed items in my therapy bag.

WINTER 1997 - 1998

A man is following me. He is part human and part animal. I open my mouth to yell but no sounds come out.

(Dream: February 20, 1998)

"At this time of year I think of suicide," I told Shirley. "The tension begins in December. My hair falls out. I have back aches and pain in my thighs. There's something I need to face. . . No! I can't say it! Something terrible will happen! I'll die!"

I flopped on the couch. My laughter filled the room. "It was at this time of year that I went to the cult," I blurted. My hands frantically rubbed my face.

"Stay here with me," Shirley said.

I sat up. My hands dropped to my lap. "I need to see your face. I need to remember what you look like," I said in a high, trembling voice.

"I won't go away. I'll hear whatever you want to say," Shirley said calmly.

My head felt enlarged and tingled with pressure coming from inside. "My father took me to the hospital where he worked, that's where it happened." I felt my body break in pieces. "I can't control myself. I can't be an adult and talk about this."

"Have you learned to remain an adult when you talk about other abuse?" Shirley asked.

"Yes. I can put what happened at home in the past and it becomes a memory. Talking about the cult is different."

"You lack control," Shirley said. "We can go very slowly."

One sunny winter day Myrna and I took Reiki training with a group of health professionals. Healing through touch, channelling the universal force of love, was an ancient tradition that attracted me. I remembered the soothing love I felt when Sally touched me. When it was my turn to lie on the table I wasn't afraid. The women placed their hands on me and my body was receptive. When I placed my hands on them, I felt great heat. A year ago this would have been impossible.

In therapy I spoke of the cult. "The memories, images, and feelings are mine," I exclaimed.

"What can help you?" Shirley asked.

"Talk to me."

"You have survived. You have a good relationship. You have good work. You've developed your aesthetic sense and love for beauty. Justice is important to you. You've kept going even though it's been hard. You have the right to get up in the morning; the right to say what you want."

"I have the right to live," I said, responding to her encouraging words. "But as much as I hate it, I believe that I need to talk about the cult."

"Yes, that's how it seems to me. You've spent a lot of energy keeping it down. You'll feel more stable after you've talked more about it," Shirley replied. "And perhaps it won't take as long as you imagine."

At home I laced up my snowshoes and set out for a trek down our lane. The cult weighed heavily on my mind. I remembered that during our visit to Ireland there were newspaper accounts of a cult that had been discovered in Belgium. Several bodies of children had been unearthed. I could imagine their fear, the fragmentation of their minds, and their despair. I wanted to sit in the snow and rock silently. That wordless lost place in my mind was my only retreat.

During our next session, Shirley asked, "What would you think if a client came to you with the material the alters report about the cult?"

"That she was hurt. That people had control of her."

"How are you feeling?" Shirley wondered.

"So sad. It was horrible. I did bad things."

"Have you tried to forgive yourself?"

"So many times. I pray. I remember that the Great Mother is in every darkness."

"I'm not surprised that you are resolving this on a spiritual level. You have your own soul. You have a right to your own life," Shirley said firmly.

"You look fierce to me," I said.

"I feel that way." She turned in her chair and looked out the window. "I say to them that Barbara has her own life. You don't own her."

Her confrontive words on my behalf stirred me deeply. I felt her care sweep over me.

I began to read a book written by a survivor of ritual abuse. I skipped the descriptions of trauma. I wanted to know the impact of her memories and how she coped. "Reading it is like being part of a conversation, but at a distance," I told Shirley.

"Perhaps it would be helpful to see what resonates and what doesn't. You're phobic about this material; reading could desensitize you."

Was relieved by her words but suddenly felt very dirty. "I'm filthy," I shouted.

"Do you know that it's a feeling?"

"No. I think it's real."

"Think about an accident in which someone is thrown to the ground, is hurt, and has bruises. She's taken to a hospital where she's cleaned and given medical care. Her body isn't dirty any longer."

"Oh," I said, grasping her meaning.

My sister and I met for a shopping expedition before Christmas. We hadn't done this for years. Her soft gray hair fell gently on her shoulders. She was more beautiful than ever. In our hours together I didn't mention therapy or the cult. She had told me that she didn't ever want to talk about Satan. We focused on the present and simply enjoyed one another.

Shirley asked me to describe what I was reading in the survivor's book. I recounted several hideous events. "How could anyone survive such brutality?"

"That seems to be a central question for you. What does it mean to survive?"

"I don't know. No one could survive it. I couldn't survive it."

"Repeat back to me, 'Don't tell me, Shirley, that I could survive that kind of brutality.'"

I said the words several times, my voice getting louder. "If I could survive it, then it could have happened." A mental door snapped open. Images raced in my mind. Descriptions of rituals tumbled out. I was sinking.

"We can set this aside for the moment," Shirley said. I breathed, eager to relax.

My sleep was disturbed by repulsive dreams of the cult, of rage, and by early morning insomnia. I took additional anti-anxiety medication and found some relief.

At the beginning of our next session, Shirley discussed some aspects of our work. "Whether or not you decide to work with alters as we explore the cult, I want you to bring your mind to this work. I want you to use your cognitive strengths. If you work as Barbara, you can remain an adult; you don't need to be a child. If you work through alters, you and adult alters can lend their intelligence. We're working to bring feeling and thought together. The separation seems extreme in you."

I felt fragile and chose the familiar path of dissociation. New and old alters worked through cult trauma supported by stronger parts. Shirley made space for them to express all of their feelings. I struggled with resistance.

"That feeling of it-never-happened continues to come up," Shirley discerned. "I wonder if you could meet with the alters that do accept the cult as part of their history and explore how they were able to do that."

I cleared a space on my desk at home and considered Shirley's suggestion. But a different question occurred to me: If I accepted the alters and their memories of the cult, then I would be complicit in dreadful acts; what the alters said may be true; my father brought me to the cult. I stopped. Daddy wouldn't have done that to me. Daddy loved me. I threw down my pencil and left the room, trying to escape.

In mid-January a vicious ice storm overwhelmed Maine. Power went out. Roads were dangerously icy. Trees snapped, leaving mounds of broken limbs. Shelters opened for people who had no heat; vouchers were distributed to people who needed food.

Myrna and I took out our candles, hurricane lamp, and camp lantern. We read to each other in the evening, played Scrabble, and even created a singing game. With our wood stove, water from a nearby town, and gas burners, we managed.

The storm created stress and hardships - and incredible beauty. Sun sparkled on the ice-covered trees, bushes, and long grasses. The world was held in webs of glistening light. A local store plastered a wall with pictures of spectacular ice scenes. Everyday talk was about surviving the storm.

"Since we began to focus on the cult material, you seem very distant from me," I told Shirley.

"It's hard for you to accept that anyone could be with you when you talk about the cult," she replied.

"Yes, that's true," I said, relieved by her understanding. "I feel exhausted. It takes so much energy to control and manage my feelings. I'm having terrible headaches again. Sometimes I just want to let go."

"What would that look like to yourself and others?"

"People would find me on the floor, shaking, moaning, maybe laughing. They'd take me somewhere. But it wouldn't help. I'd be given medicine and sent home in a few days."

"I understand that it's hard for you. What about mini-collapses, like extra bed rest or more pauses in your day?"

"Yes. The day I spent in bed last week did help."

We decided to make room for alters who had more feelings about the cult. Barbara Davis emerged. "How could God have allowed such things to happen? I wanted to be a nun and give myself to God, but inside I felt filthy. Now I know that other parts felt that they belonged to the cult. Where is God? Without God, there's nothing."

"Is there someone inside who could help you?" Shirley asked, responding to her despair.

Barbara Davis listened. "Sister told me to turn to the God of sadness. Yes, I can do that."

After the session I felt a powerful compulsion to rush home and cling to rosary beads and medals. I wanted to prove my love to God. I wanted to feel safe.

Barbara Davis and I agreed to work together at the next therapy hour. I told Shirley about the holy cards, medals, statues, and prayers of my childhood. "I loved the God who cares for the lilies in the field, for the sparrows and lost sheep, but I belonged to Satan." And then, a new awareness broke into consciousness.

"He descended into hell. Those are the words of the Apostles' Creed. If Jesus went into hell, then he was with me in my hell. Jesus was in hell with me. There's nowhere he hasn't been. God couldn't change the cruel, violent acts of people, but God was with me. I tried to prove my love to God, but I didn't need to. God's love can't be earned. The lilies receive nourishment just because they are."

I moved forward on the couch, pointing my finger at the imagined cult. "You tried to take God away but you couldn't. God was there. God never abandoned me. God is stronger than you."

My eyes closed in exhaustion. I heard Shirley sighing.

I looked at her. "The cult seems less powerful. Before, they were. . . the powers of darkness."

"Yes," Shirley said. "You've been wrestling with these questions all of your life."

"As a child I lived in a world with God and didn't know how to relate to anyone else. For me, God was a Holy Man in heaven. He was also the wind and the rain. Sometimes I believed that God was lonely. I had childish notions of God for a long time. Understanding myth and symbol changed that. More changes occurred with feminism. I left the church and eventually came to believe that everything is a manifestation of The Great Mother."

"This is only the tip of the iceberg," Shirley said. "We are deconstructing your religious experience, peeling away what was essentially a reaction formation and finding the core of integrity."

I stopped by the lake to think about her words, how the experience of believing myself to be evil contributed to an intense dedication to the spiritual life. I glimpsed the extremes in my thinking; everything was either totally evil or wholly good. Memories of my meanness and unpredictable cruelty to others came to mind along with memories of generosity.

"Jesus and Satan are powerful archetypes in western culture," Shirley said at our next visit. "Most of life is lived in between. You can be good and you can also hurt other people. We're trying to weave together both experiences in your life."

I followed her eyes to my hands, and I saw that my right hand was twisting something into my left palm. The gesture was entirely unconscious. "You appear to be twisting a nail in your hand," she said. I nodded and folded my hands in my lap.

SPRING 1998

> I watch an androgynous figure shaping a
> clay pot with great care. She shows me
> pieces of clay that need to be broken
> before they can blend into the pot.
> Another woman spreads illustrations of
> the pot on a desk. Outside, she shows me
> where the ground is fragile and warns me to be
> careful.
>
> (Dream: April 24, 1998)

Shirley observed that for most of my therapy I sit with my arms lifted with my hands between my waist and my neck. "I think of it as similar to what happens when a person is hypnotized and can lift their arms for a long period," she explained.

"I hadn't noticed it. My arms don't feel tired."

"You're in a trance state," Shirley said.

At home I made music on a new keyboard. With a kind of kinesthetic memory, my fingers glided of their own volition over the keys, recalling the practice of many years ago. The sounds were mellow; the pace slow. I played love songs from the thirties, pleased by Myrna's appreciative murmurs. Shirley said that I was reclaiming my music after wrenching it free from those who used it to hurt me.

I played freely now, at one with the child who learned the scale on her grandmother's piano; with the adolescent who mastered the organ at the local skating rink; with the youthful nun who provided musical accompaniment for community hymns; and with the young mother who tapped the keys for her children. I was able to enjoy music without fear because it was no longer a trigger that catapulted me into flashbacks.

One Friday morning I felt thoroughly disoriented. "What can you do to help yourself?" Shirley asked.

"I can change my position, stand up and walk." The movement helped and I found solid ground.

"I don't want to fall into terror," I said. A mental image of slipping into a constraining terror startled me. When these painful feelings held me, like a tightly closed bag, I had no perspective, no way of identifying a particular feeling as one among others.

And then I fell into a hole.

It happened one Tuesday afternoon. I sat across from Shirley grappling with the difficulty of integrating cult material. Suddenly, overcome with confusion, I couldn't differentiate between Shirley and me. My hands covered my face. My mind vanished.

Resting on the couch I slowly recovered enough stability to speak. "I feel like I lost my mind. I had no ground. No point of reference."

"You felt no gravity," Shirley said.

"I need to create mind, a strong ground for myself."

"You have a rich, bright mind but trauma interfered with attachment. Without attachment you weren't able to develop the world of language that develops mind. You're learning the language now in the context of our relationship. It takes time, but you're learning."

She shared with me a recently published article on hysterical psychosis. My pen raced over the pages underlining passages that described me to myself: dramatic onset, volatile affectivity, thought disorders which disappear when emotional control is achieved, hallucinations and delusions. I learned that hysterical psychosis sometimes has a dissociative foundation, that it could be seen as a dissociative state.

"This research is hopeful," Shirley said, as we discussed the article. "It suggests that as we continue to work through the dissociation that psychosis will diminish."

"Placing psychosis within the context of trauma and dissociation reduces a terrible fear. Perhaps I'll be able to trust the workings of my mind after all."

I mulled over these things as I drove to St. Mary's Abbey, a monastery I had not visited in over twenty years. I made a detour and drove to the house where Sally lived. No one was home. Bright clumps of sunny daffodils and red tulips caught my eye; a weathered bird feeder swung from a tree. I saw the garden with Sally's eyes, watching for the promise of each new Spring. Some of her ashes were here, helping life to bloom.

It was almost nine o'clock when I settled into the quiet guest house near the monastery. When my alarm rang at five a.m. I dressed quickly and walked through the dark woods to the abbey. This was Holy Week, the period during which the Christian Church remembered the passion, death, and resurrection of Christ. The psalms, canticles, and scripture readings wove suffering and joy, light and darkness into a single web.

The chapel was filled with light. The grill that traditionally separated the sisters' choir and the public section was gone. I looked at the large crucifix which revealed the mystery of acceptance that opened to resurrection. About fifty nuns entered. They wore long white choir robes over their shorter, modified habit. Some of them carried meditation benches or kneeling pads. Most of them wore sandals or sneakers.

The bells rang. We stood together to join in ancient prayers of praise and thanksgiving. Later, during the Eucharistic Liturgy I walked forward, right palm open, and received the bread of communion. Drinking from the chalice I felt the sorrows and hope of the world. All suffering, all hope was one.

I felt slight headaches accompanied by tingling sensations. The alters were switching. Some wanted to directly experience this peaceful chapel; others, disturbed by an atmosphere of ritual, sought internal protection. Barbara Davis moved easily into meditation. Tears wet her cheeks. She would never have this communal life of prayer and work, but she could inspire a spirit of contemplative living in the personality system, just as Teri helped the whole system grow into healthy sexuality, and Jeannie nurtured the capacity for play.

Sister, too, slipped into prayer. Reflecting on "the Word made flesh" - God becoming human in Jesus - she took her first steps toward accepting her body. She was ready to let go of the role she held in the system which was to deny the very existence of the body. Now that all parts of the system were remembering and healing past trauma, they didn't need her protection. Catching sight of the sisters in their work clothes doing the routine labor of the farm, Sister appreciated the goodness of physical ability and sadly accepted her own losses.

Jeana's grief was also palpable. She had longed to create a family steeped in faith and spiritual practice. "I wasn't able to give my children a religious tradition, but I believe that they will find their own way," she wrote in our retreat journal.

I looked forward to evening prayer. Now the chapel was dim. A sister lit a votive candle before the statue of Mary. The day drew to a close in subdued tones of blue and mauve.

Cecilia emerged to join the sisters in prayer. "Guard me as the apple of your eye. Shelter me beneath your wings." I heard her wish that she could have participated in comforting rituals like this, not the sadistic ceremonies of the cult. I reminded her that my childhood and adult life did include beautiful rituals and that when she's integrated she'll feel them as part of her life as well.

I walked through the night woods to the guest house, filled with awe and gratitude. "Mary, Mother of Mercy, is always with me. She blesses me with grace and compassion. Just as I am forgiven, I also forgive those who hurt us. We are all broken. Pray for us always, Mother of Sorrows."

I drove to Maine with chanting of the sisters' choir in my heart. Shirley was waiting for me. She listened as I described the profound richness of the retreat and the changes I perceived within. "I feel close to you. There's no part of myself I'm afraid to show to you." A deep smile warmed her face. We would walk this journey together until there were no more steps.

In early evening I turned into our driveway. The beauty of the thick woods, sprawling meadow, and throbbing ocean astonished me even after fifteen years. The porch light was on. I saw Myrna move from her chair at the sound of my car. Molly and Maeve leapt to the window. Myrna opened the door for me, love rising between us. I entered the warmth of our home and walked more firmly into the present.

EPILOGUE

> I find a lost child on a deserted street.
> I wrap her in a blanket and take her home.
>
> (Dream: June 6, 1998)

My therapy with Shirley inched forward. With her strong support I gradually came to accept the need for anti-psychotic medication and consulted with a psychiatrist. This was an extraordinarily difficult step but I could no longer ignore the presence of a mild psychosis underlying the dissociation. The doctor confirmed the diagnosis and I began to take a low dosage drug. Almost immediately my mind cleared. The world no longer appeared threatening and unpredictable. I could talk about my history without being flooded by overwhelming emotion and was able to accomplish even more work in therapy. With an understanding of my psychosis and the help of medication I came to a deeper acceptance of myself.

One March morning when the late winter sun flooded the therapy room Shirley asked to speak with Protector. The words tumbled out, "I am Protector."

She went on, "Can I speak with Big Barbie?"

"I am Big Barbie."

Shirley asked for Margie, Chair, Al, Billy, Jeannie, and Hope. The response was the same.

My eyes filled with tears. "There's nobody here but me," I said.

I felt an emptiness inside and a loneliness for the companions who had peopled my life. I would never again hear their voices, or watch their ideosyncratic behavior. At the same time, I felt I had climbed to the top of a mountain and breathed rarified air.

Sadness was the prevailing mood. My mind felt quiet; my body felt whole and connected. Shirley reminded me that there would be many more feelings.

I also felt fragile. "I'm thinking of an egg," Shirley said. "There's no hard outer shell, only the thin membrane to hold it together."

This was a wondrous moment, a miraculous beginning.

Change continued. My relationships became even more precious. Myrna and I were more deeply intimate and the bonds with my children were stronger. I felt more trusting with friends and colleagues. No longer apprehensive about laughing in bizarre ways, I could walk through the supermarket with ease; I could chat with friends and strangers without fearing that they saw a damaged, bruised face.

My own journey had nourished my work as a clinician. My compassion had deepened; I felt an enlarged understanding of human suffering, and increased capacity to respond. My mind was open and free.

I was amazed at how different it was to feel a solid place developing within myself. It was the experience of an integrated self, an "I". With the experience of one self, I slowly began to weave multiple strands together and tell a coherent story of my history. Remarkably, I experienced the story as mine!

I came to accept the traumatic memories that the alters disclosed. Working my way through the images of the cult I found my way back to the profound obliteration inflicted by my father. In accepting the reality of the cult, I opened to a place of deep knowing within myself and was miraculously able to find my own power. I believed that all the memories of the alters conveyed essential truths about my life.

I feel more rooted in a spiritual life. Light and darkness are one. I no longer feel driven to prove I am good, nor am I degraded by believing I am filthy. I feel a certain grace in being an ordinary woman trying to love well; and feel profound gratitude when I reflect on the intricate, interconnected MotherSoul in which I live.

Pictures of Mary grace my study wall alongside images of other Goddess figures. A Celtic cross stands on my desk. The Navajo Beauty Way Prayer rests on my windowsill. Pictures of Myrna, my children, grandchildren, sister, friends, and pets remind me of the streams of inspiration, love, and sustenance that flow into my life.

I reach for my photo album and select a picture of my parents on their wedding day. It slides easily into a wooden frame. I look at them and see the beginning of my own story. I accept them now as the limited, distressed people that they were and thank them for whatever goodness they brought into my life. Prayers for them rise easily in my heart.

Closing my eyes, I remember the child I was. I call her name, draw her close to me, and lift her onto my lap. She smells like the lupine and daisies of a fresh summer morning. Her soft body nestles into me. With love, I bend to kiss the scars upon her face.

ABOUT THE AUTHOR

Barbara Hope is a clinical social worker in Down East Maine and an adjunct faculty member of the School of Social Work, University of Maine. She holds degrees from Boston College, Harvard University and the University of Maine. Her two decades of peace work have included travel to Guatemala, Nicaragua, Hiroshima, and Dachau. She is the editor of *A Faith of One's Own* (Crossing Press, 1986). She is the mother of four adult children and has two grandchildren. She lives with her lesbian partner in Jonesport, Maine.